I SAID I WOULD DO IT,

NOW WHAT DO I DO?

I SAID I WOULD DO IT,

NOW WHAT DO I DO?

PROGRAMS FOR WOMEN'S GROUPS

V. Elaine Strawn

ABINGDON PRESS
Nashville

I SAID I WOULD DO IT, NOW WHAT DO I DO?:
PROGRAMS FOR WOMEN'S GROUPS

This book is printed on recycled, acid-free paper.

Library of Congress Cataloging-in Publication Data

Strawn, V. Elaine.
    I said I would do it, now what do I do?: programs for women's
groups/V. Elaine Strawn.
        p.   cm.
    ISBN 0-687-00254-0 (alk. paper)
    1. Church meetings.   2. Women in Christianity.   I. Title.
BV652.15.S77   1994
254'.5—dc20   94-22982

Most scripture quotations are from the New Revised Standard Version Bible, Copyright 1989 by the Division of Christian Education of the National Council of the Churches of Christ in the U.S.A. Used by permission.

Those noted GNB are from the Good News Bible—Old Testament: Copyright © American Bible Society 1976; New Testament: Copyright © American Bible Society 1966, 1971, 1976. Used by permission.

94 95 96 97 98 99 00 01 02 03 04—10 9 8 7 6 5 4 3 2 1

MANUFACTURED IN THE UNITED STATES OF AMERICA

To my guides,

Sheila Voris Wild
and
Gladys Blaine Strawn

CONTENTS

PREFACE

My partner is a librarian, and I often hear this: "We get so many requests from our patrons for program ideas for an upcoming meeting. They promised to do one, and now they don't know what to do. We don't have resources specifically for programming, so I drag out every book and article I can find, and offer them a chair. I don't have time to brainstorm with them, and it isn't very helpful in the end, anyway! Why don't you write a resource book?"

I looked through the resources, and my librarian is right. There are some resources from the United Methodist Women's Division, and some from Church Women United, but few others are available. Program chairwomen feel lost and confused. Then when they refuse to continue in that capacity for another year, the nominating committee panics. No one wants to do it. It takes too much effort and time to gather resources, ideas, and speakers. How do we plan a challenging program for the most difficult audience in the world: our families and friends?

What follows is a resource guide with some suggestions for program planning and implementation. Included are a full range of skits and discussions, warm-up exercises and events. One fully developed program is offered for each month. Four extra program ideas center around highlights of the Christian women's year. I hope they help to make program planning enjoyable.

THE ART OF PLANNING

There is no right way to plan a program, or a programming year, but it is necessary to take some time to consider the people to be involved, the time allotted, and the objective to be met. These things give us a basic outline to follow and tell us something about what we need in order to achieve our purpose.

Over the years, the answers to five simple questions have given me most of the information I need, and I offer these for your use. Again, there are no right and wrong answers. The most important things to keep in mind are the consistency of your own group and the objective you hope to meet.

1. What is required? How often does the group meet? Are you planning for the whole year, or for a single program? How organized must you be to fit your own personal style? How much detail is necessary in your planning notes to make you feel at ease with the process?

If you are planning a whole year of programming, you may want to make up a chart that gives general notes for each individual meeting. In this way, you and those working with you can put your dreams on paper, get a glimpse of the whole vision, plus allow some time to begin making those specific telephone calls, inquiries, and arrangements required by the more complicated programs.

Schedule Overview

(1) Date: (2) Date:

    Theme: Theme:

    Program Style: Program Style:

    Location: Location

    Time: Time:

    Devotions: Devotions:

    Refreshments: Refreshments:

(3) Date: (4) Date:

    Theme: Theme:

    Program Style: Program Style:

    Location: Location

    Time: Time:

    Devotions: Devotions:

    Refreshments: Refreshments:

2. What have people done in the past? Are there notes from past years? What were your favorite programs? Ask members what programs they remember. Does a resource list exist? Will the membership be the same as last year? Does the purpose of the group remain the same?

Let me add a note about complexity here. Try as we may, we cannot quite eliminate the essence of competition when it comes to programming. We do not want to be defeated or to feel inept.

When I was in junior high school, I played the trumpet. The instructor used Herb Alpert as an example of a musician. He said, "It takes more talent to carry off simplicity well than to perform masterpieces in a mediocre fashion." That was a very important lesson. Years of preaching also has taught me that the more simple sermons are the ones people remember—not because people are dull, but because simplicity embeds itself in our minds in a way that more complicated things do not.

3. What possibilities exist? What resource people do you know who can do a presentation? What is the makeup of the group? Do you have a committee to help? Do you want one? A Brainstorming Chart may be helpful at this stage. It helps to make a list of all the ideas and people who come to mind. Remember, the main principle behind brainstorming is that you make no judgments as you write. Just get all your ideas down on paper. Evaluation comes later.

Brainstorming Chart

Year's Theme:

Programs most remembered	Style
1.	
2.	

People and groups that do programs	Style
1.	
2.	

Helpful numbers and Speakers' Bureau list

1.
2.

4. What would you like to see happen? After you have answered all the other questions, you are ready to pull together your memories of the past, your ideas, your possible resources, and your evaluations. What do you think is possible? What do you think would work? Why? Circle realistic options from your brainstorm list. How many different formats can be included? Make a planning log, and plan for diversity. Too often, we find ourselves comfortable with a particular format or plan. This is your chance to introduce a fresh approach to the group's life together.

Planning Log

Focus of group:

Number of meetings:

Time allotted for the program:

Distribution of meeting styles:
_____ Group discussions   _____ Book reviews   _____ Skits
_____ Guest speakers   _____ Special/Current issues

---

5. What help do you need? It is important to know your own limitations, preferences, and time constraints. There is no righteousness in being a workaholic. Use your committee. If you don't have one, ask others to help you. Discuss each person's special talent, and assign her to that slot. It makes everybody happy. Share those areas everybody hates. It makes it more fun.

Planning Committee Members: Area of Responsibility:

_____

_____

_____

_____

_____

_____

Finally, make up a meeting plan. Make it as complicated or as simple as your comfort level will allow. But write it down. We are so busy in this world that we can't remember what we have promised to do. We want to do so much in such a short life. Recording things on paper helps everyone's clarity and increases retention. We put it into our brains twice: once when we say "yes," and once when we write it down.

Most important, have fun! If you are not enjoying what you are doing, look over your list again. What can you change? Who can you ask to help? How can you simplify things or make them more challenging? You are your own best resource.

Individual Meeting Planner

Name of Group: _____

Date of Program: _____ Time: _____ to _____

Number of Participants: _____ Time Allotted to Program:_____

Program Title:_____

Objective:_____

Devotional Material: _____

Devotion Leader: _____

Program Leader: _____

Participants: _____

Refreshments:_____ Provided by:_____

Set-up and Restoration Committee: _____

_____

Sequence of Events: 1. _____

2._____

3._____

4._____

5._____

6._____

Items Needed: 1. _____ 3. _____

2._____ 4. _____

Notes:

Individual Meeting Planner--Example

Name of Group:_____*Mary-Martha Circle*_____

Date of Program: ___*Oct. 11*_____ Time: __*7*___ to ___*9*___

Number of Participants:_*4* Time Allotted to Program: *45 minutes*

Program Title: _____*"The Seasons of Our Lives"*_____

Objective: __*to recognize change and God's leading*_____

Devotional Material: _*Ecclesiastes 3*_____

Devotion Leader: _*Ruth Smith*_____

Program Leader: _*Susan Thomas*_____

Participants: _*Sally Shock, Norma Jeffers*_____

Refreshments: _*pumpkin pie*_ Provided by: _*Jean Stormer*_____

Set-up and Restoration Committee: _*Susan Thomas, Jean Stormer,*___

*Linda Cline*_____

Sequence of Events: 1. _*Annnouncements*_____

                            2. _*Devotions*_____

                            3. _*Skit*_____

                            4. _*Discussion*_____

                            5. _*Refreshments*_____

                            6. _*Clean-up*_____

Items Needed: 1. *Baseball & Bat*____ 3. *Desk*_____

                     2. *Baseball uniform*____ 4. *Bible*_____

Notes: *Rehearse at Sally's house on Saturday at* 1:00 *p.m.*
            Contact the custodian to unlock the church parlor

CYCLE OF MONTHS

Introduction

The programs that follow are intended to be used as examples. They are blocked into an agenda only for convenience of presentation.

The few quick steps that follow will make this book easier to use.

1. Pick a format—one that facilitates your objective and relates to the time of your meeting and the comfort of the group. Feel free to change the order to meet your own needs.

2. Pick a focus that meets your objective and the group's needs:
    A. General meeting
    B. Special day/Holiday
    C. Church women's calendar

A basic program is provided for each month, and a few suggestions are made for tailoring that program to a holiday in that month, if you so desire. Additional resources are provided at the end of the book.

3. Pick a style. What style best fits the members of your group? Pick from the options suggested, plugging them into your meeting format, or write your own.

A. Guest speaker   D. Activity   G. Games

B. Book reviews   E. Tours   H. Parties (holiday)

C. Group discussions   F. Skit/Plays

The programs in the book use skits, group discussions, activities, and presentations. Other suggestions are made, but they are not primary focuses, because each group's resources are different.

I hope that, given these steps, the programs that follow will be easy to adapt to your own setting.

JANUARY

Objective

To open the new year, to remember the leadership of Dr. Martin Luther King, Jr., to celebrate the New Year's fresh start.

Introduction

The word *January* comes from Janus of the Roman calendar, the god who had two faces—one to look to the past and one to look toward the future. The color is white, the flower is the carnation, and the gem is garnet.

Program

Gathering and Announcements

Warm-up Exercises

"Getting to Know You," "Massage," "Gifts"

A Fresh Start

Sing: "There's a Wideness in God's Mercy"

Read: (Three women read the texts.)

Leviticus 25:1-13, 18-22, 33-45, 55
Exodus 23:9-12 or Deuteronomy 15:1-15
Matthew 18:21-35

Explain

God commanded the Israelites to honor a Sabbath every seven years and to honor the Jubilee year every fifty years. On each fiftieth year, all was forgotten—debts, servanthood, foreclosures. Everyone was free to start again, to make a new beginning. God's plan operated in cycles, creating a balance: work/rest, poverty/wealth, alienation/home.

We could benefit from some of this balance in our world. Such a system of dynamic equilibrium could eliminate our current imbalance in power and wealth, in development between the First and Third Worlds. Probably, it would have eliminated much of the warfare and strife that has plagued our world.

The Leviticus plan was not perfect. Israelites were treated as servants, foreigners were treated as slaves; male slaves were freed at the Jubilee, while women and children remained the property of the master, unless they belonged to a male slave.

Following this, Jesus' parable gives us a chance to laugh at people's greed, as well as be challenged by this reminder to forgive.

Act

Take some moments to list some concerns left over from last year: for example, the time your contribution was not appreciated, the cutting remark someone made. Make separate lists for your church group and for your friends or family. Look over your lists. Do any of those concerns seem funny now? Scratch those off. Are any of them still hurting you? Let's look at those.

✎ Are there any that can be removed? Circle them and make a note about how and when to resolve them.

✎ Are there any that you are not yet ready to let go? Write them on a separate piece of paper and date them. Fold the paper and put it in your purse or pocket. Vow to take that paper out during your prayer time, every day for the next thirty days. Pray for the people involved and for yourself.

21

At the end of thirty days, ask yourself whether you have let go of the issue. Do you need to do something about it? Pray about this. Allow God to guide you to the action that is best for everyone involved.

When you are finished with this issue, crumple the paper, throw it away, and pray a prayer of thanks. You may want to reread Matthew 18:21-35.

Sing: "Help Us Accept Each Other"

Reflect

Spend some time remembering the life events of Martin Luther King, Jr. (A list is provided at the end of this section. You may want to make copies, or put it on the board and go over it together.) His life is a prime example of one who challenges people to forgive, to grow, to accept one another in love. Are there others who should be mentioned? You might want to mention some in the church/community/nation who have helped with this dream of unity and justice.

Prayer (You may want to use the
Serenity Prayer here, instead)

O Great Jehovah of the Israelite clan, we too are your people—women whom you have called by name. Strengthen our resolve to do that which enables your community to grow in love and service. Teach us how to forgive, and remind us to do it. Inspire wisdom among us, so that we can understand which differences are real issues and which result merely from fatigue and misunderstanding. Encourage us as we learn. Make us strong in wisdom, strong in forgiveness, strong in diversity, and strong in love. Amen.

Refreshments and Fellowship

Alternative Program

If you want to have a full-day or an overnight retreat to begin the new year, expand this program by adding a few more warm-up exercises ("Shakes," "Team Effort," "Blindfolded," "Trust," "Acting Out," "Guess the Leader," "Meditation").

Begin each segment of the retreat with one of the scripture readings. (Add Jonah 4:10-11, Luke 7:41-43, and Matthew 18:23-35.) If planning for the year is one of your goals, use the charts in the "Art of Planning" chapter, and divide into working groups: Devotions, Programs, Refreshments, Special days, and so on.

If you are installing officers at this meeting, ask them to join the leader at the front of the room. Introduce them and their office duties. Ask if they have specific goals and what help they need. Then follow an order of installation. Dedicate their service at the end of this time, and sing "A Charge to Keep I Have." Have a time of appreciation for retiring officers.

Add a Personal Resolutions segment to the retreat. Ask members to write down any five resolutions. Then ask them to cross off one they used last year. Next ask them to cross off the one they added just to make it five. Then ask them to cross off the one someone told them they should do, but that they don't feel is necessary. Now, of the two that are left, ask them to circle one and keep it with them. During a prayer time with the group, dedicate these personal goals.

Prayer

All Knowing God, as we begin this new year, you know what troubles us and what gives us joy. You know what makes us feel guilty and what makes us free. You know, better than we, what we need and how we need to grow. We offer these promises, our covenants with you over the coming year. Guide us, direct us, make us strong, and help us to grow. In Jesus' name, Amen.

An Outline of the Life of
Dr. Martin Luther King, Jr.

1929—born, Atlanta, Georgia (January 15)

1948—graduated, Morehouse College

1951—graduated, Crozer Theological Seminary

1955—earned Ph.D., Boston University

1955-56—led Montgomery, Ala., bus boycott

1957—Gallup Poll showed him as one of the most admired religious leaders in the world.

1957—founded Southern Christian Leadership Conference

1958—began voter registration in the South

1958—wrote *Stride Toward Freedom* (Harper & Row)

1959—developed nonviolent education programs and conducted school integration pushes

1960—founded Student Nonviolent Coordinating Committee and helped organize sit-in movement

1961—conducted Freedom Rides in Albany, Ga.

1962—established SCLC Citizenship Education Programs

1963—*Time* magazine "Man of the Year." *Time* called him "the unchallenged voice of the Negro people and the disquieting conscience of the white."

1963—involved in Birmingham, Ala., Movement and March on Washington

1964—wrote *Why We Can't Wait* (Harper & Row)

1964—received Nobel Peace Prize (youngest recipient)

1964—helped pass the 1964 Civil Rights Act

1965—led Selma-to-Montgomery march for the right to register to vote

1965—helped pass the Voting Rights Act of 1965

1966—involved in the Chicago Movement which led to Chicago Operation Breadbasket

1967—called for peace in the Vietnam War

1967—involved in Cleveland Movement, helped elect Carl Stokes mayor

1968—helped organize Poor Peoples' Campaign

1968—assassinated, Memphis, Tenn. (April 4)

FEBRUARY

Objective

To understand the love of God and the way we are to love one another; to expand our knowledge of African Americans' contributions to our country's history and to remember Presidents George Washington and Abraham Lincoln.

Introduction

The word *February* comes from *februarius* and *feruare,* Latin words meaning "to purify." The snow associated with this month "purifies" the earth. This is a time to examine the purity of our hearts. The color is red, the flower is a violet, and the gem is an amethyst.

Program

Gathering and Announcements

Give Me a Pure Heart

Most often, we think of love in romantic terms. We send frilly cards and chocolates and roses to the ones we love. God speaks of the heart as a thing to keep pure; it is the organ that governs our wills and our spirits. There is much in the scripture about love and clean, or pure, heartedness.

In the large group, read each of the scriptures aloud and ask the women to help summarize each in a phrase. Then ask, "What does it tell us about love?" Write the comments on newsprint or on the board (Examples are given).

1. Deuteronomy 6:4-9 (Love the Lord your God . . . .): how we relate to God; the text sets our priorities.

2. Matthew 5:43-48 (We must love our enemies.): how we relate to the conflicts of the world; the text challenges us.

3. First John 4:7-21 (Beloved, let us love one another.): how to live in our community; the text tells us the source of love.

Next, divide the group into clusters of four or five. Ask the members to read First Corinthians 13 together. This is a text we all know well, though it may govern our lives. It is a beautiful chapter, but if we were writing it for our own lives this afternoon, what would it say? Ask the groups to rewrite the text. (An example is given at the end of the section.)

Group I rewrites verses 1-3:

(What are the special things you can do of which you are most proud? What talent or power would make you feel that you could move mountains? What mountains are there to be moved in your life? What acts of charity do you do? What would constitute a truly big gift or act for humanity?)

Group II rewrites verses 4-7:

(In what areas do you have trouble with love? Are any of those listed problems for you? How do they play themselves out in your life? In what area are you most tempted to give up? In what problem is it hard to imagine faith, hope, or patience succeeding?)

Group III rewrites verses 8-10:

(Name the talents of which you are most proud.)

Group IV rewrites verse 11:

(What things did you do differently when you were a child: speech, emotions, thoughts? Now you are grown. How are you different? Name the ways.)

Group V rewrites verse 12:

(What things are you aware of that God probably sees clearly, but on which you have a limited perspective? How well do you know or understand yourself?)

When everyone is finished, come together and read the paragraphs, then read verse 13 together in its original.

Sing: "Give Me a Clean Heart"

Prayer

Indwelling Spirit, cleanse our hearts of their biases and their prejudices, so that we may be free to love all who come across our paths in this journey of life. You who can see all that we are, help us to know ourselves. Build up our insecurities, heal our hurts, quiet our fears. Love us for all that we are and all that we hope to become, that we may be your ambassadors of love and hope and peace. Amen.

Alternative Program

Frederick Douglass said, "Find out what any person will quietly submit to, and you have found out the exact measure of injustice which can be imposed upon him." If you choose to concentrate on Black History Month, have people list famous African American people from memory, then have them answer the quiz included in the Additional Resources section.

You may want to have a guest speaker on African American issues/history/culture. Or you may want to review a book, such as James Cone's *Spirituals and the Blues* (New York: Seabury, 1982). In this case, choose only one text to use in the devotions, then sing "We Are Climbing Jacob's Ladder," "Go Down Moses," or one of the spirituals reviewed by Dr. Cone in his book.

Prayer

Loving Jesus, so many of those you have called into service have given so much. We have named but a few here this day. We thank you for their lives and their great contributions to our world and its freedoms. Inspire our insight and determination, so that we may see the prophets working among us today and strive to help them, rather than question and hinder their progress. For your sake, Amen.

First Corinthians 13: A Paraphrase

I may be able to speak so eloquently that poets and presidents turn around and stare, but if my words are not uttered in love, they are worthless. I may be comfortable in speaking in front of huge crowds, I may have an unusual understanding of economics and politics and be an aeronautical engineer, but if I don't do it all in love, I am nothing. I may be the world's greatest philanthropist, with statues and halls named for me, and even be willing to give my second kidney for transplant to save a life, but all of this does me no good if my spirit is not loving.

Love is willing to wait for change, and do so kindly; love is not controlling or uppity or proud; love is not rude or self-centered or easily upset; love does not keep a tally of another's wrongs in order to use it against them at a later date; love hates what is unjust and full of lies and greed; love is happy only when justice and truth exist in the world.

Love is determined—it never gives up, no matter what odds oppose it: the state, the police, the school, the church, even family. Love's faith, hope, and patience never run out.

Love lives on forever. All the charismatic speeches come to an end, and people with especially spiritual gifts will lose their ability to use them, because all our specialties and areas of expertise are only part of the picture. When the Kingdom of Heaven comes, we will know what truly special is! We will understand perfection!

When I was young, my talk and emotions, and even my thoughts were those of a young person. Now I am an adult. I have matured.

Regardless of this, I still see with only my limited human vision, full of its stubbornness and prejudice and confusion. When God's perfect will is revealed, I will be able to see beyond the end of my nose. I will see God face-to-face. The things I know and understand now are only limited partial truths; then I will see the whole picture and understand the universe, as well as myself.

In the meantime, I can rely on three things: faith, hope, and love; the one I count on most is love.

MARCH

Objective

To recognize Women's History Month and International Women's Day, and to remember the call of the scriptures.

Introduction

March is named for Mars, the Roman god of war. In the original Roman calendar, the year began on March 25. This was the time when all leases for homes and farms were signed. Not until the Gregorian calendar was the beginning of the new year moved to January 1.

The color is green, the flower is the daffodil, and the gem is the aquamarine. This is the month of the equinox, the beginning of spring, when days and nights are of equal length as they make their way toward summer.

Program

Devotions

Sing: "Go Down, Moses"

Read: Exodus 13:20-22; 14:19-20

Sing: "Oh Mary, Don't You Weep"

Pray: The Lord's Prayer

A Woman of Persistence:
An Interview with Sojourner Truth

(Three women are needed: IN—the interviewer; ST—Sojourner Truth; PR—the postscript reader.)

IN: Good Afternoon. We are so lucky to have with us a powerful woman whom I have wanted to meet all my life. Please welcome Ms. Sojourner Truth.

ST: Thank you. I'm frankly surprised to be here.

IN: I must start with the question I hear most often. Is "Sojourner Truth" your real name?

ST: Course it's my real name. God give it to me. I hear God isn't just "He" anymore, so I got to be careful. God call me "Sojourner" because I was to be travellin' up and down the land showin' people their sins and bein' a sign to them. "Truth" came from the truth I was supposed to be speakin' to people. You know, "Thou art the master, and thy name is Truth."

IN: Were you born with that name?

ST: Oh no, honey. My mamma and daddy called me Isabella. My daddy was called "Baumfree," meaning "straight as a tree." And he was. That's where I got my tall, skinny shape. We "belonged"—can you imagine belongin' to somebody?—Oh, my Lord! I hear there's still slaves in some parts of the world! We got to stop that, now. Anyway, we belonged to a tavern owner in New York. He made us live in a dark, damp cellar. We slept on straw cots on the old muddy floor. It's a wonder we didn't all die of rheumatism. Finally did kill my mama, Mau Mau Bett.

IN: Did you have any family life to speak of?

ST: Course we did! We were slaves, not animals. Even lots of animals got family life. Mau Mau Bett used to take us outside some nights. We sat under the stars. They're for everybody to share, you know: slave and free, man and woman. She taught us that God hears whatever we say and that we should always ask for God's help. We learned the

Lord's Prayer from her in Dutch, the language I learned first.

IN: One of the horrors of slavery was the splitting of husband and wife, children and parents. You were sold away from your parents when you were nine years old?

ST: Sure was. The master died, and his family had to split up his property—us included. My folks was too old to be any use as slaves, so they got set free so not to be a bother in their old age. They kept livin' in that old damp cellar. Later Mau Mau Bett died there of fever sores and palsy. Twelve years after that, my daddy died. He'd been set out. I found him froze to death in an old run-down shack.

IN: But you and your brother were sold.

ST: Yes, Ma'am. My brother Michael and my sister Nancy had been stolen when they were little. Almost killed us. My brother Peter and I was put on an auction block—my mother's worst nightmare. They said I had a bony frame, so Nealy bought me for $100.

IN: Did life improve?

ST: Lord, no, Child. I couldn't speak nothin' but Dutch and they couldn't boss in nothin' but English. I still have scars from beatings I got when I was ten years old. Master's ropes tore right into my skin. I worked all winter in no shoes.

IN: That's when you began really praying hard, asking God to deliver you from the Nealys. How did God respond?

ST: Well, first I prayed for my daddy, and he limped up one day. Then a new man bought me, you can't imagine how it feel to be bought and sold like so much flour. This time life was better. He set me to unloading boats and hauling supplies to his tavern. That's where I picked up this pipe [she holds up a pipe]. I've had a lot of complaints about this thing. Shorten my life and all. But I lived to be eighty-six years old, and here I am again. Guess it didn't do me too bad.

IN: You finally learned English from the dockers at the wharf.

ST: Not so's any lady would speak it, though.

31

IN: When you were thirteen, John Dumont bought you. You stayed with him until you took your freedom.

ST: "Took it"—that's right. Nobody give it to me. Dumont was kind, called me "Belle," said I could work better'n any six others. I never questioned him, didn't question slavery much. All day, I did as he said; then at night I went out to the willows, bargainin' with God, just like Mau Mau Bett taught me.

IN: What changed your mind about slavery?

ST: First I fell in love with a slave from a nearby plantation. His master beat him near to death to get him to stay away from me. You see, if we had any children, they'd have belonged to *my* master instead of his, so his master married him off to a woman on his own plantation. Dumont gave me to a slave named Thomas. I birthed five children.

IN: What was the second thing?

ST: Slaves were to be set free in New York on July 4, 1827. Dumont promised to set me free a year early, because I'd been such a good slave. But when I hurt my hand, he refused.

IN: That's when you decided to run away.

ST: That's when I bargained with God. If God helped me get away from the master, I'd be good. If God didn't help, I wouldn't. God told me to leave two or three hours before daylight. So I grabbed my baby and left. Then I just asked God to show me where to go.

IN: You have stated that God showed you the home of the Quaker couple who took you in.

ST: They gave me a bed. I didn't know what to do with it, so I slept under it! They were good to me, protected me when the master caught up with me. That's when I met Jesus— standing between me and the burnin' heart o' the Lord, telling me to forgive the white folks that had abused me so.

IN: We're coming to a great victory in your life. When you discovered that your son Peter had been sold illegally, you filed a complaint with the Grand Jury, and you won! The slave owner was arrested and you got your son back. You must have felt proud.

ST: I felt like I'd got my son back. There was nothing else to do.

IN: Then you moved to New York and caught up with your sister and brother. You worked at a women's refuge, and got involved with a fanatical man named Matthias. The authorities accused you of aiding him in the poisoning death of one of the members of that group.

ST: You interviewers *do* like to dig in the dirt, don't you? I hear your political campaigns are *something* anymore! In my time, a charge was dropped and forgotten when a body was acquitted. I even got $125 for damages to my character!

IN: I'm sorry for bringing it up. From New York, you began to use your chosen name and traveled through the country. You really became quite famous for your preaching and singing.

ST: I couldn't read the Bible. I had children read it to me instead of adults. *They* could read without having to interpret it all the time. My main text was always, "When I Found Jesus," though. People always wanted to hear that one.

IN: Harriet Beecher Stowe said of you, "I do not recollect . . . anyone who had more of that silent and subtle power which we call personal presence that this woman."

Frederick Douglass and William Lloyd Garrison sought your company and called you "Aunty Sojourner." Many people spoke of your "warm heart and tongue of fire." Let's talk about Akron for awhile. The "Ain't I a Woman" speech was probably your most famous. But the people who gathered at that suffrage convention in 1852 were not too happy to see you. They actually hissed when you came in, and when you got up to speak.

ST: For some reason, many people couldn't see that the women's movement and the abolition movement were tied together. Oppression is oppression, no matter what the issue. So I walked in and sat quiet long as I could. The chairman was under terrible pressure not to let me speak. But there came a time when I just couldn't hold my tongue anymore. When those preachers started misrepresentin' God, I had to stand up.

IN: May I?

ST: Certainly.

IN: I quote:

"That man over there says women needs to be helped into carriages . . . . Nobody ever helped me into carriages, or over mud puddles, or give me any best place. And ain't I a woman? Look at me. Look at my arm. I have plowed and planted and gathered into barns, and no man could head me, and ain't I a woman? I have born'd five children and seen them sold off into slavery, and when I cried out with a mother's grief, none but Jesus heard—and ain't I a woman?

"That little man in black there—he say women can't have as much rights as men because Christ wasn't a woman. Where did your Christ come from? From God and a woman! Man had nothing to do with him!

"If the first woman God ever made was strong enough to turn the world upside down all alone, these together ought to be able to turn it back and get it right side up again; and now they is asking to do it, the men better let them!"

You even *thanked* them for listening to that wonderful speech.

ST: Just because a few people're actin' ugly don't mean I don't have to be polite. I knew we had to keep stirrin' it all up, or else it would take a very long time to get it started up again.

IN: Of course we must address the horrible meeting in Indiana, where they accused you of being a man.

ST: People'll think up any excuse so's not to hear the truth.

IN: After the Fugitive Slave Act of 1850 passed, you called Frederick Douglass into account: "Frederick, is God dead?"

ST: No, not really. Frederick and I were always interested in the same thing. That law making it illegal to help escaping slaves cut us to our souls. But I had to remind Frederick that even this was no cause to think we had to take over God's job. Violence doesn't bring justice—it brings more violence.

IN: When mobs threatened to burn the hall in Angola, Indiana, where you were to speak, your friends dressed you in military garb and escorted you, but you wouldn't take a weapon.

You said, "I carry no weapon; the Lord will preserve me without weapons. I feel safe even in the midst of my enemies; for the truth is powerful and will prevail."

ST: When what you got works, don't let it go.

IN: In the spring of 1864, you left for Washington, D.C. You were seventy years old.

ST: I needed to talk to President Lincoln. We talked, but it was the poverty of the slaves rushin' across that old Mason-Dixon line that kept me there.

IN: You stayed and worked—teaching hygiene and nursing, finding work for folks, fighting the raiders.

ST: That's when it hit me that slaves needed land. If the railroads got land out West, why not slaves? So I set out again, getting people to sign my petition.

IN: You sat in streetcars with white people and refused to be put off; you fought child labor and capital punishment. You took on the temperance struggle, and you worked for equal pay for equal work, long before it was fashionable.

ST: Fashion never mattered beans to me, honey. What hurts me most is how many of those struggles got to be fought over and over. You'd think people'd get tired of bein' so stubborn!

IN: Many of those fights are still our issues today. You went home to Battle Creek and tried to register to vote. You kept stirring it up, but were frustrated by the reluctance of others to do any stirring.

ST: My health got worse. A doctor even grafted some of his own skin onto my fever sores to save me. But I got more and more aware of how important it is to forgive, and the more forgiving I got, the more serenity I had.

IN: We need to close now. I don't know how to thank you for all the contributions you have made in the world, for your determination, and courage, and insight.

ST: It's all in the fight for justice. Keep stirring them up, honey.

PR: POSTSCRIPT: Sojourner Truth died at 3:00 A.M. on November 26, 1883. She reassured her friends: "I'm not going to die, honey, I'm going home like a shooting star."

Read: Luke 18:1-8 (the persistent widow)

Prayer

Lord, make us persistent: persistent in the face of injustice, persistent in the face of hunger, persistent in the face of poverty, persistent when combating ignorance, even our own. Amen.

Refreshments and Fellowship

Alternative Program

If you choose to concentrate on Spring, center on beginnings. Have some eggs lying around. Eggs are the beginning of so much—the life of a chick, the making of a cake, breakfast—a tiny miracle in such a thin shell, a miracle of creation.

In spring, we probably are more aware of the blessedness of creation than at any other time: days are getting longer, crocus and daffodils are coming up, with a promise of much more. How often we read the reflections of people who look back on their lives and wish they had taken a few more moments to smell the flowers, to look around in awe, to notice the beauty.

Devotions: Sing "This Is the Day"

Often, we remember to pray but forget to praise. God needs to be thanked for all the miracles of life, and we need to spend time being thankful. Creation is ours to enjoy for only a short time. The act of thanks puts the whole of creation in perspective. The psalmist was good at this. Read Psalm 104.

Prayer

O Great Creator of all that we see and hear and touch and smell, words do not exist to express our wonder. We thank you for your miraculous beginnings—for eggs and buds and blooms and greenery. Help us to be good stewards of your creation, for the short time it is in our care. Amen.

Sing: "All Things Bright and Beautiful"

Program

Invite a guest speaker to bring a collection of ornate eggs, or have the group decorate eggs—for themselves or for the church or community. Be creative. We adults permit ourselves to have too little fun.

APRIL

Objective

To celebrate Easter, to learn about eternal life, to have fun with April Fools' Day.

Introduction

The word *April* comes from Aprilis, or Aphrodite, the goddess of love and death. *Aprerire* means "to open." The color is crimson, the flower is the daisy, and the gem is a diamond.

Program

Gathering and Announcements

Sing: "Love Divine, All Loves Excelling"

Fun with April Fools' Day

April Fools' Day comes to us from the Roman Veneralia, the festival of Venus (Aphrodite), when all types of foolishness were acted out to venerate the goddess. It symbolizes love's victory over logic.

Love takes us all to the heights of grandeur and the valleys of utter foolishness. We never feel so grand as when we are doing a task for, or with, someone we love. Then we are at our best. We also catch ourselves wondering why, as we do something a little ridiculous, or even dangerous, because our loved one has requested it. We drive to an airport at 4:00 in the morning, or through the horrors of rush-hour traffic on a highway under construction; we peel the skins off our grapes, or shave celery. We work overtime until we are exhausted, and then announce, "If you ever ask me to do this again . . . !" Like the Romans, who on this day ordered each other around on meaningless errands as proof of their love and devotion, we too are caught being foolish sometimes.

Break into groups of four and tell one another the most foolish thing you remember doing in the name of love. Have fun with this. (Example: "When our son missed the schoolbus, I hopped in the car and drove him to school because he had a report due the first period. I didn't take time to get dressed, so when the engine stalled on my way home, I had to decide whether to sit in the car and wait for someone I knew to come along, or get out of the car in my bathrobe and slippers and walk to the nearest telephone. I felt so foolish!") After ten minutes, ask for stories from the groups and take time to enjoy them.

Next, remind people of the psychological "game" we sometimes play: "If you *really* loved me." Sometimes this is done in fun; sometimes it is very serious. Again ask the small groups to think of examples from their own lives. (Example: "If you really loved me, you wouldn't make me go on this business trip alone!") Allow ten minutes, then share examples.

Sometimes we feel very foolish. Sometimes we are frightened. Love can be a very manipulative thing. Love also can give meaning to our lives.

Sing: "O How I Love Jesus" or
"What a Friend We Have in Jesus"

Comment

We are continually making decisions about the "sanity" of requests made by our loved ones. "Should I really do all the housework myself, when I am working full time at another job?" "If I don't like his mother and don't want to be around her very much, does it mean I don't really love him?" "Will the kids be impaired for life if they can't go on this trip?"

We are always judging the requests of our loved ones. "Am I being a fool to do this?" Our friends usually have lots of advice for us.

Jesus made continual requests and demands of the disciples. Sometimes they were even couched in the same words: "Simon, if you love me, feed my sheep" (John 21:15-17). The disciples had to make life decisions when they didn't understand his requests; sometimes they found themselves roaming around with outcasts. More than once, they balked at Jesus' demands. What must it have been like to walk with this man for three years, to spend days on end at his side? What must it have been like when he began talking about his impending death?

Make a list of "foolish" requests Jesus made of his disciples at the end of his earthly life. How did they respond? How would you feel? How would you respond?

Read

1. Get a mule for me to ride. Mark 11:1-7
2. Get a room for our Passover meal. Mark 14:13-16
3. Let me wash your feet. John 13:2-8
4. Go with me to Gethsemane and *stay* awake. Mark 14:32-42
5. Do not stop them from arresting me. Matthew 26:51-54
6. Believe that I am risen from the dead. John 20:24-29
7. Go into the world and make disciples. Matthew 28:16-20

Love is a paradox. It asks us to hold on—to Christ, to our spouses, to our families and friends. Love asks us to hold on—with all our belief and trust and faith—*and* to let go. To cling to love until we become secure, until we can understand without question, until we feel firm enough to loosen our desperate grasp—this is to kill love. And the disciples had to face this. Jesus asked them to believe unbelievable things, to follow unreasonable demands, and then also, to let go. For in hanging on, we lose life, Jesus said. Paul called it being "fools" for Christ. If we follow only worldly standards, this may be so. But it is not true if we place our love and trust in the Christ of the Resurrection.

Read: Luke 10:25-28 and John 11:25-27

Sing: "Jesus Is All the World to Me"

Pray

Jesus, we have promised to love you until the end. But often, we don't know what loves requires. We ask ourselves whether we are being wise when we follow some of your demands. Fill us with an abiding faith in your power to conquer any odds we encounter, including death. Help us to be wise in our actions and firm in our love. Amen.

Sing: "Blest Be the Tie That Binds"

Alternative Program

If you choose to concentrate on the women at the tomb, read the text in John 20:1-18. Ask yourselves how the women must have felt—their fears, their hopes, their disbelief.

Become Mary. What would you have done? Would you have done anything differently? Would you have believed, especially when Jesus wouldn't let you touch him? For an example of how Mary may have felt about the whole experience, see "Letter to a Sister," in *Fifteen Services for Small Churches* by Strawn and Nees (Nashville: Abingdon Press, 1992).

MAY

Objective

To honor the mothers of our faith, and to celebrate Memorial Day by remembering those who have gone before us, leaving us a rich legacy.

Introduction

The word *May* derives from Maia, or Maria, the goddess of spring, who brings forth life. The color is pink, the flower is the lily, and the gem is the emerald.

Program

Gathering and Announcements

Meal (possibly a Mother/Daughter banquet)

Devotions

Each time Jesus met a woman, he was breaking the law. The world of men and the sphere of women were completely separate in the society in which Jesus grew up. Jesus sent women out as witnesses to a society that wouldn't accept a woman's testimony in court; he taught them in a society that punished men for educating women. He touched the woman with the flow of blood—a woman defined as untouchable and unclean. The first person to whom Jesus confided his messiahship was a woman; the woman at the well was a person whom Jesus should not even have acknowledged. This Jesus is the Love of God, incarnate and reaching out to us.

Pray

Jesus, our friend and our Savior, we thank you for sharing your mission and your ministry with us. Against the teachings of your elders and the religious leaders of your time, you reached out to include our mothers. You called them into ministry with you and established their worth in God's kingdom.

Today, you reach out to include us in your ministry. Make us strong in the face of exclusion and denial. Keep us focused in the presence of obstacles. As we strive to follow the paths our mothers trod, give us courage and strength and wisdom. Amen.

The Mothers of Our Church: "Who Am I?"

Four women serve as panelists for this game-show format; they are seated at a table facing the audience, and have a list of questions in front of them. The leader serves as Hostess and is seated at a table across from the panelists, also facing the audience. She invites each "Mystery Guest" to enter and sign the register (large enough for the audience to see). The Hostess then shows the pad to the audience and invites the Mystery Guest to be seated beside her. At this time, the panelists' questions begin.

Mystery Guest #1: Saint Brigit (c. 450–523 C.E.)

Hostess: We welcome our Mystery Guest No. 1. Please enter and be seated.

Guest: Thank you.

Panelist 1:   Good evening. May I ask where you were born?

Guest: I was born in Ireland in 450, at Fochart, in County Louth.

Panelist 2:   Were your parents famous?

Guest: My father was a nobleman, but my mother, she was but a slave.

Panelist 3:   Did your father take good care of you?

Guest: Alas, no, my darlin', he didn't. Me father, he sold me to a Druid priest—you know who they are, the tree worshipers—whilst I was but a child.

Panelist 4: Did you become a Druid yourself?

Guest: I can see you don't be knowin' much about Druids, there. Women don't become Druids, they become Witches, a term that had a very different meaning in my time, you know. But, to your question, I didn't become. He did the becomin'. I made a Christian of him.

Panelist 1: How did *you* become a Christian?

Guest: Well, me father tried to marry me off to the King of Ulster, but the good king saw that my heart belonged to Jesus, so he let me go.

Panelist 2: Did you remain one of the faithful?

Guest: Deary me, Lass. They made me a saint after I died. They tell me I'm second to ole St. Pat himself.

Panelist 3: What are you most proud of in your life?

Guest: It was *afraid* I was, that you'd be having us braggin' on ourselves. Well, I founded the first religious community of women in Ireland. That I took pride in. But . . . .

Panelist 4: Certainly, please continue.

Guest: But the most important thing was my sacred wells. You know water was real important to Jesus. We had a well in Kildare where people came for healing: They got their sight back, their wounds were healed—people came from all over to be refreshed. There's nothing stronger than the powers of God, you know. And you can't get people to understand the compassion of Jesus, lessen you got some yourself first. You have to take care of folks' bodies and senses. They used to get such relief in the water!

Panelist 1: I have a guess.

Hostess: Yes?

Panelist 1: Are you Saint Brigit, the Abbess of Ireland, the one they call Mary of Gael?

Guest:	One and the very same, Child.
Hostess:	Thank you for coming. Will you sit here and welcome the others with us? (She directs the guest to be seated in the front row of the audience.)

Mystery Guest #2: Hildegard of Bingen (1098–1179)

Hostess:	Will Mystery Guest No. Two please enter.
Panelist 1:	Good evening. Shall we begin with your birthplace?
Guest:	We can begin there, but that is one of the least important details about me. I was born in Germany in 1098.
Panelist 2:	May I ask your vocation?
Guest:	That is difficult to answer. I will try to shorten it. I entered a Benedictine convent at age seven and took my vows at age fourteen. At age thirty-two, I began having visions from God, so I began to paint my scivas, a way to be able to share God's messages with my sisters.
Panelist 3:	May I ask . . .
Guest:	Tut, tut, I'm not nearly through. I made studies of all the things of creation: animals, plants, minerals, elements, the circulatory system, and the malfunctions of the human brain. I guess that would make me a scientist. Then we needed worship at the convent, so I wrote hymns and poetry and plays. I was also considered quite an accomplished musician. Some called me the Sybil of the Rhine.
Panelist 4:	Who were your friends? Anyone we might know?
Guest:	Well, Dear, I wouldn't know who you know, but I did count Bernard of Clairvaux among my friends. He and I mobilized the forces for the Second Crusade. King Henry III and Pope Eugenius III came to me for advice. Both of them probably were dead by the time you were born.
Panelist 1:	What do you consider your greatest accomplishment?
Guest:	Well, in 1136, I was made an abbess. We later moved to Bingen, and I founded several other convents.

	You see, convents and monasteries were the only light in a very dark and ignorant world. I believe you call that time the Dark Ages.
Panelist 2:	I believe your life has come into prominence again in our era, thanks to several devoted scholars. The paintings of your visions were so far ahead of your time. God truly showed you mysterious and wondrous things. Were you canonized in the fifteenth century? Are you . . . ?
Guest:	Yes, I am Saint Hildegard, Abbess of Bingen.
Hostess:	I knew you would recognize this guest. Hildegard, you certainly have made an impression on the world. Thank you. Now, would you join the other women in the audience?

Mystery Guest #3: Anne Hutchinson (1591–1643)

Hostess:	Mystery Guest No. Three, would you join us, please?
Panelist 1:	May we know where and when you were born? Why do I always have to ask that question?
Guest:	I suspect it is due to thy primary position, Madam. I was born in Lincolnshire, England, in 1591.
Panelist 2:	Did you live there as an adult?
Guest:	No, my father was a clergyman, so we fled the religious persecution of that land. In 1634, we traveled to the colonies and settled there. I was a nurse and proved to be quite popular.
Panelist 3:	Is it nursing for which you are most remembered?
Guest:	No, I presume it was for my religious stance that thee invited me to this place. You see, I believe that a person is redeemed through faith, not through good deeds.
Panelist 4:	That is what the apostle Paul wrote.
Guest:	The leaders of Boston church called it Antinomianism. When I accused them of relying too heavily on their work and not on faith, it split the community.

	I had the governor on my side, but they had his deputy on theirs.
Panelist 1:	How was the dispute resolved?
Guest:	When the governor lost the election, he was replaced by the deputy. Then some of my followers refused to take up arms to defend the colony, so the governor charged me with sedition. Boston church charged me with heresy and excommunicated me. I was banished in 1638.
Panelist 2:	Did you go back to England?
Guest:	Things were worse there, and travel was not as easy in those days as it is now. I acquired some land from the Narragansett Native Americans, what you now call Rhode Island.
Panelist 3:	Did you go there alone?
Guest:	No. My husband and my numerous followers went with me. There, we established a community based on true religious freedom.
Panelist 4:	I believe your name is Anne Hutchinson? I remember reading your story in a history of America.
Guest:	Yes. I am Anne. I hope religious freedom is still being honored today. Thank thee for inviting me here.
Hostess:	Thank you for coming. Now, would you join the others? and would our final Mystery Guest join us here?

Mystery Guest #4: Antoinette Brown Blackwell (1825–1921)

Panelist 1:	I am going to start differently this time. What is the thing for which you are most famous?
Guest:	Well, I don't know that I am famous. If I am remembered, it is because I was the first woman to become an ordained minister in the United States.

47

Panelist 2: What denomination were you?

Guest: When I graduated from Oberlin Seminary in 1850, I met so much resistance that I preached in any church that would have me. In 1852, however, I became pastor in the Congregational Church in South Butler, New York. Later, I became a Unitarian.

Panelist 3: Why did you decide to enter the ministry?

Guest: God called me. That is why anyone enters the ministry, isn't it? I had been speaking in the Congregational meeting in my hometown in Henrietta, New York, since I was a child.

Panelist 4: Did you tackle specific issues in your ministry?

Guest: My colleague Elizabeth Cady Stanton once stated that when people who resist social reform have no other excuse for their actions, they bring up the Bible. They interpret it to be in favor of greed, drunkenness, slavery, and capital punishment. Then they use it against the rights of women. She was right in her analysis. I could not sit by and allow the Bible to be so abused.

Panelist 1: Can you give us any more hints?

Guest: Well, I married into the famous Blackwell family. When I married Samuel, I became the sister-in-law of both Elizabeth Blackwell and Lucy Stone. He and I had six children. I wrote some books—maybe you would recognize some of them: *The Social Side of Mind and Action* and *The Sexes Throughout Nature* . . .

Panelist 2: Now I remember! We studied your life in my women's group one month. You are Antoinette Brown Blackwell, right?

Guest: Yes. I am The Reverend Antoinette Brown Blackwell.

Hostess: We appreciate all who helped in our program this evening, and we hope you will stay around. I'm sure some of the women will want to speak with you later.

Closing Prayer

O God of the ages, You have been with us in every generation, giving us strength, surrounding us with community, leading us in your paths. There are still campaigns to wage in our day. Give us strength to act. Make of us leaders who bring about your justice and compassion in this era. Amen.

Alternative Program

Have a fellowship dinner and include an informal time of worship, reading John 4:1-30. Use the devotional material from the original program, and sing hymns: "How Like a Gentle Spirit," "The Care the Eagle Gives Her Young," "Woman in the Night," and "Oh Mary, Don't You Weep." Read Rachel Conrad Wahlberg's "The Woman's Creed" as a closing.

JUNE

Objective

To begin the summer with time for quiet reflection, to rest, meditate, and be refreshed.

Introduction

The word June comes from the goddess Juno, the protector of women and marriage. Thus June came to be known as the month of marriages. This is the month of the summer solstice, the longest day of the year in terms of sun hours, the time when the earth is midway on its journey around the sun. The color is purple, the flower is the rose, and the gem is a pearl.

Program

Gathering and Announcements

Sing: "Morning Has Broken"

Meal and Fellowship (This might be a breakfast meeting)

A Time for Quiet

Sing: "Spirit of the Living God"

Exercise: "Shakes," "Pulling Together," "Side Stretch," "Massage"
(see Additional Resources)

Directed Meditation

Allow time for quiet today. The meal is over, and there has been time for exercise; now is the time for quiet contemplation of our

God. It is the time to allow ourselves to be touched by God in the silences and in the reflections. Slow your body down as much as possible. Let your body relax. Don't worry about going to sleep, it's OK. Let your shoulders fall. Let your legs relax. Get as comfortable as possible in your seat. Listen to your breathing and the breathing of the woman next to you. The psalmist wrote, "Be still, and know that I am God" (46:10). Feel the presence of God all around you, filling this spot. Take a few moments to feel God with you and inside you.

Read: Jesus Calming the Storm (Mark 4:35-41)

Jesus calms our fears, just as he calmed the storm. But we don't often allow him to do this for us. Like the disciples, we think we must get through everything alone, using our own strength and know-how. Take your pulse, you don't need to count accurately. Just be aware of the power of your heart. You don't make it run. You couldn't even stop it. There are many things we do not control, though we like to think that the whole community rests on our doing or not doing something crucial. Listen to your thoughts for a moment. Is your schedule trying to interfere with your relaxing? Put it out of your mind. Each time something barges into your thoughts, put it out again. Just do this for a few moments. Relax . . . (Pause one minute).

Read: Jesus Gives Us Rest (Matt. 11:28-30)

Jesus gives us rest. God commanded the Israelites to rest every seventh day of the week, every seventh year of the decade, and every fiftieth year of the century. God commanded rest! Allow yourself to settle further into your seat. Which muscles in your body are the tightest? Give them your permission to relax. Take off your watch and place it on the seat beside you, or someplace where you won't forget it. How does your wrist feel without it? Does it still feel as if you had it on? Feel the seat holding you up. This is how God supports us, if we allow it. Become as heavy on the seat as you possibly can. Is it holding you? Relax, and let the seat do its job. Relax . . . (Pause one minute).

51

Read: Alone Time (Matt. 14:23; Mark 1:35; Luke 22:41; John 6:15)

Jesus took time to be alone, time out from service, time out from his disciples and from those who needed him. When was the last time you planned some time to be alone—completely alone? Did you feel guilty about it? Did you have an enjoyable time? Does it frighten you? Do you do it regularly? Spread out as much as you can. Relax. There is no one here to call you, no telephone to ring and distract you, no one demanding that you meet their needs. Only you know that you are here—you and God. Take some moments to listen to your own thoughts. Try to focus them on Jesus' time of prayer. Relax and feel the free space around you. Fill all the space you have. It belongs to you. Relax . . . (Pause one minute).

Read: Prayer (Phil. 4:6-7)

Take some absolutely quiet time now to pray, to think, to rest. Talk to God. Do not forget that prayer is both talking and listening. God may have some things to tell you. God may not find you alone very often! When it is time to come back into focus, you will hear the music . . . (Pause 3 minutes).

Sing: "Sweet, Sweet Spirit in This Place"

Conclusion

Does anyone want to share anything with the group? Did you relax? Were you able to clear your mind of all those things you need to do? We are such doers in this society. We have a plan for every moment, from the beginning of the day until its end. Before we go out into the world again, let us read one more admonition from Jesus.

Read: Lilies of the Field (Matt. 6:28-34)

Prayer

God of Silence and God of Peace, we get so tired in our daily routines, but we can't think what to leave out. Somewhere deep inside, we know you care for us, just as you care for the lilies of the field, but we cannot seem to lose our need for control. Just as strongly, we believe that we alone hold the world together. There are so many demands on us and on our time. God be with us now. Remind us of Jesus' example and teach us to relax—not once a year, but daily and weekly. In the name of the Calmer of Storms, we pray, Amen.

(Note: Don't forget to take your watches.)

JULY

Objective

To remember Independence Day, and to honor the women patriots of our country.

Introduction

July is derived from the name of the well-known Roman Emperor, Julius Caesar. The color is green, the flower is the water lily, and the gem is the ruby.

Program

Gathering and Announcements

Sing: "America the Beautiful"

Meal (Picnic food may be featured)

Prayer

As we gather to celebrate and to remember, be with us, O God of Wisdom and Strength. As pride for our native land rises within us, remind us also of all the other lands that belong to you. Fill us with a patriotism that will energize us in the struggle to work for more equality and justice. Guide us as you guided the Israelites. Make us a people of justice, wisdom, and compassion. In Christ's name, Amen.

Dedicated to Her Country:
A Mock Convention

Set up the room as for a political caucus or campaign speech. Place a podium in the front center of the room, with four chairs behind it. Two chalkboards or easels display the names of past honorees and new candidates. Women may want to make posters advertising their candidate. Decorate the room with red, white, and blue banners. A spirit of fun and "pompous" rivalry should be in the air. These nominations occur in the sixth year of a fictitious convention: the "Annual Patriot of the Year Contest." Have a list of the previous winners at the front where all can see. Three women will sit at the front, ready to present their nominees. Assign three other women to sit in the crowd to heckle slightly and to present nominations from the floor. Distribute pencils and slips of paper to everyone present, so they may vote later.

Leader: Thank you for coming this afternoon. It is time once again to choose our Patriot of the Year. As you will notice, our past honorees have been listed:

The first year, we remembered the Algonquin princess Pocahontas (1596–1617), called Matoaka ("the playful") by her people and Rebecca by the Christian community into which she was baptized and married. She was chosen because of her help in interceding for trade and peace between the English and the Native Americans—a truly strong woman who helped establish our lives here.

The next year, we elected Abigail Smith Adams (1744–1818), whose letters so impressed us. We noted her courage and independence while running the family farm (and raising five children) in the midst of siege and epidemic, while her husband John was in Philadelphia and England during the Revolution. This courage was met later by her wisdom as she served at his side in England, Paris, and the White House. It is too bad she did not live to see her son in the Presidency.

55

Following this, we elected Susan Brownwell Anthony (1820–1906), the first and only woman to appear on our U.S. currency.—I remember that we all left with a silver dollar that year! This daughter of an old colonial family first taught children, then went on to instruct adults on abolition, temperance, and suffrage—work which she supported with her energetic speaking tours across the country. Such a tireless worker for justice!

The fourth year, we chose Anna Eleanor Roosevelt (1884–1962) as our Patriot. From volunteering in Jane Addams' Settlement Houses, to the national tours she waged for her husband's New Deal, she was a crusader for civil rights and social reforms. In 1948, as the delegate to the U.N., she received a standing ovation for her part in drafting the Declaration of Human Rights. A true crusader!

Finally, we come to last year's Patriot, the first black woman elected to congress: Representative Shirley Chisholm of New York (b. 1924). Emerging as a leader in the field of child care, she became Brooklyn's voice for the rights of women and minorities, an advocate for employment and education opportunities in the inner city. She is a leader in our century.

Now comes the question of this year's Patriot. Our committee has selected three candidates, each a woman of character. Each committee member will present her nominee, then we will entertain nominations from the audience.

Voice from Audience: Why can't we all just present our ideas together? We could lay them all out, then everybody could vote.

Leader: We want to preserve some decorum in this meeting. Rest assured, we intend this to be a fully democratic process, but I will have order! Now, would the first member present her nominee?

Woman #1:   I am here to nominate a powerful woman from the early part of our nation's history. The daughter of a lord, she came to the Colonies from England in 1638, becoming a powerful landowner and serving as an executor for Governor Calvert. She proved her courage when she restored calm and raised funds for mutinous soldiers by selling lands belonging to Lord Baltimore, the Proprietor! She demanded and received a vote in the state assembly. In 1651, she left Maryland to follow her brother Giles to Virginia to establish an estate named Peace. I nominate one of the most influential people in the development of the Colonies: Margaret Brent (c. 1601–1671).
(*Applause.*)

Leader: Thank you. May we have the next nomination, please?

Woman #2:   Yes. This afternoon, I would like to place in nomination the name of the first woman to earn her medical degree in this country. Immigrating from England in 1832, she studied medicine in order to place a strong barrier between herself and marriage! Her application was considered a joke at first, but 20,000 people watched her graduate from Geneva College of Medicine. She studied in Paris for awhile, then in 1857, she opened the New York Infirmary for Indigent Women and Children. Eleven years later, she and her sister opened a medical school for women in the United States, and later, one in England. She emphasized hygiene and preventative medicine, opposing experimentation on animals. I would like to nominate Dr. Elizabeth Blackwell (1821–1910).
(*Applause*)

Leader: Thank you. Here, don't forget your sign. I believe we have one more nomination.

Voice from Audience: You said you were going to open it up!

Leader: We won't forget you.

Woman #3:   Thank you. My nominee was the fifteenth of seventeen children born to ex-slaves. She went to school between cotton-picking seasons until she won a scholarship to Moody Bible Institute. She intended to become a missionary to Africa, but instead became a teacher in the South. She opened a school for girls in Florida, selling cakes as a means of support until a wealthy industrialist took an interest. In 1923 her school joined with the local boys' school to become Bethune-Cookman College, of which she served as president for many years. An appointee to the National Youth Administration, she worked to develop opportunities for youth in education and recreation. I would like to nominate Eleanor Roosevelt's close friend, Mary McCleod Bethune (1875–1955).
(*Applause*)

Leader: Thank you. Now, as we promised, we open the floor for nominations. I recognize the woman over here.

Audience Woman #1:   I don't know why nobody ever remembers Frances "Fanny" Wright (1795–1852). Maybe I am just partial because she was Scottish too. She was a friend of LaFayette, traveled with him through the U.S. in 1824, and discussed the problems of slavery with Presidents Jefferson and Madison. In 1825, she settled in our country and worked to provide money to settle slaves in Tennessee, as a step toward emancipation and colonization outside the U.S. One group did settle in Haiti in 1830. Against public objection, she lectured against slavery and monopolies, and in favor of free education, birth control, and emancipation of women. I want to put Fanny Wright's name into the ring.
(*Applause*)

Leader: Are there any others?

Audience Woman #2:	Yes, I have one.
Leader:	The chair recognizes you.
Audience Woman #2:	I would like to place into nomination the name of Fannie Lou Hamer (1918–1977), the granddaughter of a slave who labored on a plantation until she was fired for trying to register to vote! She helped organize voter registration throughout the U.S. and led the black Mississippi delegation to the Democratic convention. She was committed to human rights and to using the voting booth as a way of achieving justice and equality, regardless of personal cost. She is a stirring Patriot: Fannie Lou Hammer.
Audience:	Fannie Lou! Fannie Lou! Fannie Lou!
Leader:	Order! Order! Please come to order. We take your nominations to heart. Are there any others?
Audience Woman #3:	Yes, oh, er, I, uh, have one, maybe. (shyly)
Leader:	Yes, please come forward to the stand, so we can hear you.
Audience Woman #3:	I, uh, think we should elect, um, Frances Perkins.
Voice from Audience:	Who?
Audience Woman #3:	Frances Perkins, the first woman appointed to a Cabinet post.
Voice from Audience:	Why?
Audience Woman #3:	I'm sorry?
Voice from Audience:	Why should we elect her? You have to convince us. It's part of the process.
Audience Woman #3:	Oh. Yes. We should elect Frances Perkins (1882–1965) because she wrote so much of the policy that rules our lives today. She drafted the Social Security Act and National Labor Relations Act in 1935, and the Wage and Hour Act in 1938. She worked with

59

Workers' Compensation legislation after investigating the Triangle Shirt-waist Company fire of 1911—you know, 147 young women workers were killed. She helped decide when we go to work, how long we stay, how much we get paid, and when we retire. I can't think of a more influential woman, let alone a more efficient Secretary of Labor. I definitely and proudly nominate Frances Perkins as Patriot of the Year.

(*Loud Applause*)

Leader: I see no more nominations. Let us recap. We have currently in nomination:

> Margaret Brent (1601–1671)
> Frances Wright (1795–1852)
> Dr. Elizabeth Blackwell (1821–1910)
> Mary McCleod Bethune (1875–1955)
> Fannie Lou Hamer (1918–1977)
> Frances Perkins (1882–1965)

I think it is time to hold our election. Will the ushers come forward to help me count? Please write on the slips of paper in front of you the name of the woman you feel would make the most outstanding Patriot of the Year. Then drop them in one of the ushers' boxes. (*As people are voting, sing "America the Beautiful," then announce the winner.*)

Leader: There are so many wonderful leaders! I am pleased to announce to you that _____ is our new Patriot of the Year. We will add her name proudly to our list of Patriots. I thank you all for your participation—democracy in action!

The Ceremony

Leader: Now, as we do every year, let us read together "The New Colossus," the famous words of American Jewish poet Emma Lazarus, which are engraved on the Statue of Liberty:

Not like the brazen giant of Greek fame,
With conquering limbs astride from land to land;
Here at our sea-washed, sunset gates shall stand
A mighty woman with a torch, whose flame
Is the imprisoned lightning, and her name
Mother of Exiles. From her beacon-hand
Glows world-wide welcome; her mind eyes
  command
The air-bridged harbor that twin cities framed.
"Keep, ancient lands, your storied pomp!"
  cries she
With silent lips. "Give me your tired, your poor,
Your huddled masses yearning to breathe free,
The wretched refuse of your teeming shore,
Send these, the homeless, tempest-tost to me,
I lift my lamp beside the golden door."

Sing: "This Is My Song"

Closing Prayer

O God of the Nations, we thank you for all the talent and leadership with which you have blessed our nation. Do not allow arrogance to grow within us. Keep us humble and attentive to your leading through the ages. Develop leadership in us, also. Make us Patriots of the Year: proud of our homeland and ready to sacrifice whatever we must in order to make it more charitable, more just, more wise and far reaching. In the name of the one who calls us into action, Amen.

AUGUST

Objective

To study peace and to commit ourselves to being peacemakers.

Introduction

August comes to us from Augustus, the Roman orator. The word August, meaning "one filled with the spirit of wisdom," was used to refer to emperors. The color for this month is yellow, the flower is the poppy, and the gem is the peridot.

Program

Gathering and Announcements

Sing: "Heralds of Christ," "O Day of Every Nation," or "O Day of Peace That Dimly Shines"

Read: Beating Swords into Plowshares (Isaiah 2:1-5)

Peacemakers: One and All

Especially during this month, our thoughts turn to ideas and visions of peace. Threats of nuclear attack or economic devastation wreck our world. When one nation reduces its determination toward aggression, another seems to take its place. Our personal lives also contain dispute: family, neighbors, landlords, tenants. The list goes on. Teachers in this field stress the importance of beginning with ourselves as we search for world peace. A world of peace, in other words, is one filled with peaceable people.

The Sermon on the Mount collection in Matthew begins with a series of the attributes of a peaceable person, one who lives graciously in the world. Six of these attributes lead to the completion of the seventh—peacemaking. It is important to spend time reflecting on our own lives. What disputes, unforgiven hurts, harshnesses keep us from being peacemakers? When we have truly taken that inventory, we need to examine the conflicts that exist in our community. How can we introduce peace into those disputes? Finally, it is important to look at our larger world. What can we do to help create a peaceful kingdom?

Using the Beatitudes as a blueprint, examine yourself and your world. In groups of three or four, rewrite the Beatitudes, making them as specific as possible to yourself. Another option is to use the example given. After each Beatitude, list ways in which you can improve in this area. Think of this as a covenant that you are making with yourself, with the other women in the room, with your community, and with the world. This is also a promise you are making to God concerning your future behavior.

(Allow 30 minutes for this exercise. Sing "Shalom Chaverim" or "Dona Nobis Pacem" to bring the whole group back together. Discuss how the project went. Ask each small group to report or to share its Beatitudes.)

Vows (Leader)

As with every commitment, we must make our vow to live by this new covenant. The Beatitudes in the book of Matthew are followed by a series of four challenges which Jesus gave to his followers. We could say that they are the marks of a Christian in the world.

Will You Promise to:

1. Be salt to your world, giving brightness to life, preserving your society from decay, adding vitality to the routine matters of life?
(Women: "We will.")

2. Be the light of the world, bringing out the bright influence of the gospel, helping to expose the latent beauty in human hearts,

calling forth brightness and song, leading your community forth
into service and usefulness?
(Women: "We will.")

3. Be a city on a hill, making sure your Christian character
stands out as an example, giving confidence to those around you,
being a shelter and a refuge for those who are lost or afraid?
(Women: "We will.")

4. Be a lamp on a stand, revealing the light of Christ to all?
(Women: "We will.")

Sing: "Let There Be Peace on Earth"

Closing Prayer (or the prayer of Saint Francis of Assisi)

God of all ages, times, and peoples, do what is necessary to turn
us into makers of peace. We open ourselves to your leading,
direction, remolding, and challenging. In the name of the Prince
of Peace, Amen.

Refreshments

The Beatitudes: A Paraphrase

1. Happy am I when I am conscious of my need of God. Even
when the going gets rough, my faith in God will not be shaken.
To nurture this faith, I will set aside time each day for prayer and
meditation. I will surround myself with people of faith who will
support my commitment to God. I will seek out those things that
strengthen my faith. Through me and others like me, God does
the work of establishing the realm of justice and truth on earth.

2. Happy am I when the injustices of the world deeply trouble
me. I will spend time looking inward at my own greed and malice,
and be honest with myself. I will also scrutinize my community
and world, better learning the needs of the community and world
around me. I will work to amend these wrongs. I will follow the
example of Jesus—the friend of the outcast and the disinherited.
When I act to do those things within my power, my soul will be
comforted and find rest.

3. Happy am I when I listen and try to understand what others are telling me, *before* I become angry. I will be gentle and considerate with those around me. I will be humble before God. Calmness and serenity are choices I make each day. When I cease to fight against the flow and humbly release my need to control, the world becomes mine.

4. Happy am I when I long for God's righteousness and equity and humanity. No matter what my current vocation, I will use it to help create a world directed by God's goodness. I will study Jesus' visions of the Kingdom of God. Each day, I will live more and more as a citizen in the realm of righteousness and justice, rather than a resident in a society of chaos and corruption. When I make this my full aspiration, all my needs will be met.

5. Happy am I when I banish feelings of revenge and spitefulness. I will monitor the state of my feelings every day and notice my reactions to life's events. I will remember that I also require the tolerance and gentleness of others. When I detect harsh or judgmental actions or thoughts within me, I will strive to replace them with feelings and actions of mercy. Only in this way will I be able to receive the mercy that others offer me.

6. Happy am I when my heart is open and free, when my motives are pure. I will take an inventory of my personality. Where there is manipulation or abuse, I will rid it from myself. I will replace these with integrity, with true vision and clear aims. With my eyes and my soul uncovered, the clouds disappear from my vision and I am able to see God.

7. Happy am I when I have done all these things and may be called a peacemaker. As an agent of reconciliation, I am following Jesus' example as an ambassador of peace. I will be active in my pursuit of all that peace requires, and I will be diligent in developing skills to carry out peaceful actions. When I do these things, I will have become a complete and total child of God.

8. Happy am I when obstacles, and even threats, impede my way. My guiding principles are not characteristics easily understood or trusted by many in the society. But I will and must carry on my dream and commitment, for I am helping to bring about the reign of the kingdom of God.

SEPTEMBER

Objective

To examine the role of stories in our lives, to look at some of the parables, and to scrutinize some of the stories we have been told.

Introduction

September comes from the Latin *septem,* the "seventh month," for its position in the original Roman calendar. The color is brown, the flower is the aster, and the gem is the sapphire. This is the month of the fall equinox, when the day and night are of equal length and the earth has completed three-quarters of its revolution around the sun.

Program

Sing: "Come, Ye Thankful People, Come"

Prayer

O Creator of the Seasons of Time, this month takes us into another fall. We are grateful for your order. We draw security from knowing that you are in control. Bless us in this time, and draw us closer to self-understanding and to your Truth. Amen.

Exercises: "Pantomime," "Helping" (see Additional Resources)

Storyteller Christ

Jesus was a great storyteller. His most effective teaching came from his personal example of living, and from the parables he told. People could understand abstract principles from those stories of everyday life, even when those principles contradicted the truths that the Pharisees had taught them all their lives. Jesus was able to get through to people in a way few teachers and religious leaders can. Think of all the idioms of our language that describe a person we can fully understand: "down to earth," "eyeball to eyeball," "got down on my level," "talked my language," "walked in my shoes." Through his stories and his parables, Jesus was able to be fully understood by the ruling elite, and also by the homeless.

Stories, or parables, provide a whole picture for us to relate to. They tell us about the world around us and how we fit into it. We are able to follow along and remember what the storyteller has said, because we too have entered into the story. Good storytellers plot out a journey, then take us with them. They paint scenes in our minds, and, whether or not our pictures are the same as those of everyone else, we follow along, getting more and more involved along the way. Have you ever heard a person tell a story so well that you had to blink twice to get back to reality when it was over? Maybe this has happened to you after reading a book? Stories are similar to shadow boxes—through a very small opening, we can see an entire world.

The sacred stories that were told to us as children were deeply embedded into our memories and souls because the vision was painted within us at such an early age. We had no choice about whether we liked the story or wanted to listen, because our powers of reason had not yet developed. We are not even conscious of many of the stories. In our minds, they change only very slowly, if at all. They are truly part of us, as surely as the identity of our parents or our birth date. Many of them were placed in our memory banks at the same time as those details. We have been living with our sacred stories as long as with our names.

Just as all of us are very complex beings, so are the stories we have included in our memories. They have several layers. For example, a very complex story is that of the garden of Eden. We first may have related to Adam and Eve as parents. Maybe when we reached primary age, we were embarrassed by their nudity. Then in older childhood, we may have wondered how one brother could have killed his sibling—though on *some* days we probably had no question or astonishment at all! A little later, we began to think about the whole universe that God had called into being. Not long after that, we entered into the debates about creation.

As women, we have always—either consciously or unconsciously—absorbed some kind of message about the value of women, and of ourselves as individuals. Are we sinful or not sinful? Are we truly to be no more than a helpmate, and what does that mean? Are men really missing a rib?

First, at about high school age, we may be conscious only of the need and desire to remain true to God, to follow God's commands. That develops into devotion and establishes our allegiance to God's direction and guidance. Most women don't begin to question, until middle or late adulthood, how much wrongdoing Eve actually was responsible for. The story has many layers of understanding. Each time we retell it, we learn new things or notice different aspects. It is the same story, but it gives us new understandings from the original experience.

Reflection (leader)

The important thing is the effect that stories have on us. Not only do they tell us about the world around us, they also determine our own behavior. They tell us right from wrong. On those stories, sometimes without even knowing it, we base our actions. Let's examine some of the biblical stories now.

Storytelling

(Ask someone to tell the story of the two builders: Matthew 7:24-27.)

What is the moral, or teaching, of that story?

(Ask someone else to tell the story of the rich fool: Luke 12:16-21)

Both parables center around builders, but their message is completely different. Both parables are stories to which Jesus' hearers could relate easily. He tells them as fables, always providing morals at the end. According to Matthew (13:34-35 GNB):

Jesus used parables to tell all these things to the crowds; he would not say a thing to them without using a parable. He did this to make come true what the prophet had said,
"I will use parables when I speak to them;
I will tell them things unknown since the creation
of the world." [Ps. 78:2-3]

Activity

Break into groups of three or four and assign stories. Ask each woman to read the parable and then tell it as a story. Ask the others to listen and remark on differences in details, then on the message they received. Each woman's storytelling style will be different. The other women also will notice different things with each telling. Assign one of the following to each group:

The Unjust Steward (Luke 16:1-9)
Parable of the Laborers (Matt. 20:1-16)
The Two Sons (Matt. 21:28-32)
The Samaritan (Luke 10:30-37)
The Good Shepherd (John 10:1-16)

Next, assign another parable. In this case, it will be the same story. It will vary only in that it was written by a different Gospel source. Again, have someone read the parable, then tell the story. Ask the others to comment on details and message.

Then ask the next woman to read from a different Gospel and tell it from that author's point. It may be necessary to repeat sources in some cases, to allow everyone to tell the story. Reflect on how the Gospels differ. Assign one of these sets to each group of women:

1. The Sower:	2. Tenants in the Vineyard:
Matthew 13:3-9 and 18:23	Matthew 21:33-44
Mark 4:1-9 and 14-20	Mark 12:1-12
Luke 8:5-8 and 11-15	Luke 20:9-16

3. Preparation:	4. Guests:	5. Debtors:
Matthew 25:1-13	Matthew 22:1-14	Matthew 18:23-35
Mark 13:34-37	Luke 14:15-24	Luke 7:15-24
Luke 12:35-40		

When the groups are finished, ask people to comment on the differences observed. How did it feel to tell the story?

Concluding Comments (Leader)

Ours was once an oral tradition, with its history passed by story from one generation to the next. The elders would tell the children the sacred stories and have the children tell and repeat them, correcting errors until each detail was correct. Some cultures still pass their heritage in this way.

Closing Prayer

Jesus, our friend and our teacher, bless our lives with stories. Inspire us and direct us through your parables of life. Just as we have practiced here this day, keep us telling your story so that we may become the elders, passing the parables of the kingdom to our children and into the future. Make us aware of the power of the stories we tell, for in our stories, we bring about the future. Amen.

Sing: "Tell Me the Stories of Jesus"

Refreshments

OCTOBER

Objective

To look at the seasons of our lives; to have fun, with change and limitation; to develop understanding that God is in control of it all and that things come in their own good time.

Introduction

October comes to us from the Latin word *octo,* meaning "eight," its position in the Julian calendar. The color is blue, the flower is the calendula, and the gem is the opal.

Program

Gathering and Announcements

The Seasons of Our Lives

During October, the leaves on the trees around us turn vibrant colors. There is a different smell in the air, and we know in our souls that the earth has begun its journey from summer toward winter. Our consciousness of the changes makes us aware of the design of God's creation.

This is also the month in which we celebrate Halloween. The ancients said that at this time of year, the curtain between life and death is most transparent. We think of ghosts, of skeletons walking, of graveyards and scary stories. In the Christian world, Halloween is the Eve of All Saints, a time when we honor the lives and contributions of those who have gone on before us. Thus, this is a good time to think of the seasons of one's life.

Sing

"Morning Has Broken" or "See the Morning Sun Ascending"
READ: Ecclesiastes 3

The Season It Came to Be

(This skit is planned in four acts, as a slice of a fictional woman's life. Have fun with it. It requires three to nine women, depending on the availability of actresses.)

Sing

"Turn, Turn, Turn" ("To everything, there is a season"—words of Ecclesiastes, music by Pete Seeger, recorded on *The World of Pete Seeger* [Columbia Records, 1973].)

ACT I: SPRING

(In a kitchen: a mother (M), dressed as an adult, and a daughter, Kathryn (K), dressed as a child who is about to go out to play. Kathryn should have a baseball and bat. K enters and walks up to the mother . . .)

M: Honey, what are you doing with your brother's bat?

K: Reverend Parker said they needed players on the church team, 'member?

M: Hum. I do remember, now that you remind me. Did your brother send you to get his bat for him? That's very nice of you, Honey.

K: No, Mom! Jimmy ain't got nothin' to do with this. I'm gonna be on the team! Spring try-outs are today!

M: Jimmy *hasn't anything* to do with this, Dear. We can work on your grammar this summer while Jimmy has baseball practice. I didn't realize he enjoyed baseball so much. I wonder when he decided to play.

72

K: Mother! Jimmy isn't gonna be on the church team. *I* am! I have my bat and my ball, and I'm goin' to the church to sign up. I'll be back before dinner.

M: Kathryn, you are not going anywhere with that tone in your voice!

K: I am! I'm going! Reverend Parker needs me!

M: Oh, Honey, who put this silly idea in your head?

K: It's not silly! I can run real fast and I'm gonna practice and be as good as any o' those ole big kids!

M: Honey, when Reverend Parker made his announcement in church, he was asking any boys or men in the church who liked to play baseball to join the church league.

K: He didn't say "men and boys." He said *anybody* who liked to play baseball. I'm goin', Momma. I'm goin'.

M: My little determined girl. There are some things people just know. We all just knew that Reverend Parker was talking to the men and boys. Little girls just don't play baseball. They sit on the bleachers with the women and cheer. That's very important, too, you know.

K: But why don't little girls play?

M: Some things just don't have an answer, darling.

K: I don't understand why girls can't ever have any fun. Some day I'm gonna. I am!

M: I'm sure you will, Honey. I'm sure you will be out there, some great season in the future.

(The women exit.)

Sing: "Turn, Turn, Turn" chorus

ACT II: SUMMER

(In an office: two women, Mrs. Simms (S), a college adviser, and Kathryn (K), dressed as a college student.)

S: Now, Katie, what can I do for you this afternoon?

K: I just wanted to get some information about graduate schools.

S: Good. You are a bright student, Katie. I'm glad you are considering graduate study. Not enough young women do. How can I help?

K: Well, most of my course is finished . . .

S: What is your major?

K: Religion.

S: An interesting field for a young woman. There are lots of career possibilities in that area for someone like you.

K: What schools exist, and where are they?

S: Well, I can think of several schools that have very qualified training programs for Christian educators.

K: Well, that's not exactly what I had in mind . . .

S: Of course. You want to become a parish assistant. I'm not certain you really need graduate school for that. I'll look.

K: No, you don't quite understand . . .

S: I think I know what you're getting at, but I must warn you, the foreign mission field is not nearly as glamorous as it sounds, dear. It is very lonely, and can be quite dangerous.

K: I want to become an ordained minister.

S: An ordained minister? But, my child, you are a young woman!

K: Yes, but I feel it is what God wants me to do.

S: Have you talked with your parents about this?

K: Yes. They were a little unnerved at first, but when they understood that it was God's call, they gave me their support.

S: Well, of course, there are *some* churches that are ordaining women, but the toll it takes on them! It is almost impossible to care for a husband and children, in addition to caring for a congregation. Most women wait until they have raised their children, and then they become parish assistants.

K: God is calling *me* into the ministry!

S: Yes, I understand that you feel that, Katie, but you don't understand how difficult it is. There are still many people who think a woman has no business in a pulpit. There are so many obstacles.

K: I know. I tried to play baseball once.

S: Excuse me?

K: Never mind. May I at least look over some school catalogues?

S: Why don't we do this? Why don't you talk with your pastor over the summer? Then when you come back in the fall, you can make an appointment with the Dean of Students. Maybe he can help. I know this seems harsh now, but I think you'll look back and thank me.

K: I think I'll just look back and realize it wasn't my season yet. *(The women leave the stage.)*

Sing: "Turn, Turn, Turn" chorus

ACT III—FALL

(In a living room: Mrs. Harris (H), the head of the church board, and Kathryn (K), in a housedress.)

H: Thank you, Kate, for allowing me to come to your house this afternoon. I thought it might be a little more private. There is always so much going on at the church.

K: Yes, I think that's how a church should be.

H: You're right. It just keeps Pastor Ellison running all the time. He wanted me to thank you for the fine job you are doing with the youth group. How long have you done that?

K: Ever since my oldest daughter entered junior high, about two years, I guess.

H: My! Children do grow up fast, don't they?

K: Before you know it. What was it you wanted to discuss?

H: It's about the youth group, actually.

K: They're such good kids.

H: Yes, they seem to be very attached to you. There was one, ah, small incident I wanted to talk with you about.

K: Nothing wrong, I hope?

H: No, not exactly. I'm sure we can clear it up. You have a child in your group, a girl, Millie Sanders.

K: Yes. She is going through a difficult time right now.

H: Yes, her mother thinks so, too. You see, Mrs. Sanders called me yesterday. She was a little upset about a conversation you apparently had with Millie about . . . private matters.

K: Millie seems to need someone to talk with. She is so confused. It may be the new school this fall. I try to help.

H: Maybe a little too much. She may be taking advantage, Kate.

K: I certainly don't feel taken advantage of. Millie is making some very weighty decisions these days.

H: There you have it. Mrs. Sanders is concerned that she is thinking about things and making decisions she has no need to be making.

K: We're talking about sexuality, aren't we? Mrs. Sanders doesn't want Millie to talk with me about those concerns.

H: Mrs. Sanders, Pastor Ellison, and myself agree in this. We feel that young girls should be thinking about studies, parties, and babysitting, rather than about other things. There is plenty of time for the other later, Kate.

K: It is normal for a high school junior to have questions about her sexuality, and about demands and "normal" behavior, June. I did at that age, and I'm sure you did, too. I haven't told her to *act!* I have just listened, and affirmed her doubts as normal. As a matter of fact, she told me our conversations have helped her to stop seeing a boy who was pressuring her. Our conversations let her know *that* was OK.

H: Well, I am glad to hear that. Still, I am not sure it is the task of the church to instruct our young people on such issues. I think Mrs. Sanders has a point. There is plenty of time for that later.

K: The church's task is to be honest with its youth. Jesus was.

H: Even so, I think we should soft-pedal certain issues. We don't want our youth to get the wrong idea.

K: You're asking me to stop talking with Millie, and with anyone else who has questions?

H: No, I am just asking you to give the group a good solid footing in Christian values.

K: That's what I thought I was doing! Have you seen a baseball around here anywhere?

H: Excuse me?

K: Never mind. I guess it's the wrong season.
(The women exit.)

Sing: "Turn, Turn, Turn" chorus

ACT IV: WINTER

(In an empty room: Kathryn's daughters, Jane (J), dressed in professional attire, and Sandy (S), dressed in a baseball uniform; Kathryn (K), holding suitcases, is older.)

J: Mother, I'm sorry I couldn't help you pack. Darrell and all the kids have been sick this winter.

K: That's all right, dear. I remember how busy a mother's life is.

J: I can't believe your house is sold. I have so many memories in this place.

K: Yes, I know, dear. I was a bit unstrung when you and Darrell suggested selling.

J: Now, Mother, you aren't sorry, are you? You forget you are seventy-five years old. You remember how hard it was when Darrell's mother needed care.

K: Yes, I do. That was hard on all of you. I understand your desire not to go through that again.

J: I know you feel well now. But a person your age needs to be in a place where there are ramps and handrails and elevators already installed, where you can age gracefully. I especially liked the place with the pull ropes in all the rooms. Is that the one you decided on?

K: No, dear, not exactly. But I am very happy with my choice.

J: Good. We just want what is best for you. Settling into a retirement home where everyone is your age and has your interests can be exciting. Think of the friends you will make!

K: I have lots of friends here.

J: I know. But it pays to be prepared. Where exactly *did* you decide to move?

K: Oh, a very pretty place. I haven't exactly seen it yet.

J: What? Sandy is allowing you to move into a place, sight unseen? Where is it? We can go look it over now.

K: Oh, I've seen pictures, and I've talked with the director over the phone. They have exactly the right spot for me.

J: How do you know without seeing it? Pictures can be deceiving. Where *is* this place?

K: It's in Puerto Rico.

J: What? You have to be kidding. You are, right? Does Sandy know about this?

K: Yes. Your sister and I have talked about this a long time, and we talked with Reverend Stevens. She thought it was a good idea, too. She knows the people who run the place.

J: What kind of retirement centers do they have in Puerto Rico? What kind of health care do they have? It's the Third World!

K: Well, it's not exactly a retirement center.

J: Oh my! Mother, what have you gotten yourself into? I should have known not to leave this up to Sandy!

K: It's a mission run by our church. I feel as if I know all the people. Our circle studied it last year. I will be teaching young women English and helping them manage their homes on a low budget. I haven't forgotten those first years with your father. But their faces all look so bright. I'm probably the one who will be doing most of the learning.

J: Mother, you are *not* going to do this. This is just irresponsible. You can stay with us until we find a retirement home you like. I just can't believe you would even consider such a thing!

K: Sometimes you remind me so much of your father. I miss him.

J: Mother, listen to me!

K: Now, dear, just calm down. I am to stay with a lovely couple. We have spoken several times. They helped to found the mission fifteen years ago. They went as tourists and were so crushed by the poverty that they stayed and have been working with the country's poor ever since. I am quite excited, actually. I wouldn't miss this chance for anything. Not even for you, my darling Jane.

J: I feel so helpless. I don't know what to do.

K: Don't do anything, dear. I am doing what I want to do. Your sister will be here as soon as her game is over. I'll spend the weekend with her, then fly south on Monday. I would love it if you brought the boys and saw me off at the airport. Here comes your sister now.

J: Mother . . . !

K: Jane, I feel I have been waiting for something all my life. Finally, it's here. This is gonna be my season, Sugar! *(to Sandy)* How was your game, dear?

(Sandy enters, takes the suitcases; all three exit.)

Sing: "Turn, Turn, Turn" chorus

Closing Prayer

O God of the Seasons, remind us who is in control. We fight against so many barriers from grocery lines, to ignorance; from schedules, to hunger. Through it all, you call us into action. We need do only what you assign and leave the rest to you. This is your world, formed according to your design. You are the Leader still. Amen.

Sing: (optional) "This Is My Father's World"

Refreshments

NOVEMBER

Objective

To honor Thanksgiving by examining our style of praise and care in thanking our most important Giver-God, to learn how to dedicate ourselves to a lifestyle of active thanksgiving.

Introduction

November comes from *novem*, the Latin word meaning "nine," the place of this month in the old calendar. The color is green, the flower is the chrysanthemum, and the gem is the topaz.

Program

Gathering and Announcements

Sing: "We Gather Together to Ask the Lord's Blessing"

How Do We Say Thanks?

Give each woman a piece of business-letter-sized paper and a pencil. Holding the paper horizontally, ask each one to write her name on the top, and under that, write four words synonymous with *thanks*, spaced out across the paper (for example: praise, gratitude, appreciation, indebtedness). When they have finished, ask them to pass their paper to the woman on their left.

Now ask each woman to write three ways in which she has practiced each of those words during the past year (for example, under praise: wrote an article in the newsletter about the youth group's commitment to the mission work camp; told Ellen how nice the altar flowers looked; sent a letter to the parish committee praising the pastor's visitation over the last three months). Pass the paper three more times, then have the fifth woman look over the list and return it to the woman whose name is on the paper.

Allow a little time for discussion and reflection. How good are we at thanksgiving? Were words and examples easy or difficult to write? Give yourselves praise for having done these things—each woman in the room has a list of twelve different things that someone has actually done this past year. Are there things on the list that you had not thought of before? Ask the women to take these home and make a commitment to do one act of thanks every month. That is not a big commitment, and examples are before us, but it is easier for all of us to *intend* to do things, rather than to actively *do* them. The nice thing about any kind of action is that its energy ripples and spreads. When we act, we begin to create a world of thanksgivers.

Read: Being Doers of the Word (James 1:22-25)

Sing: "All Creatures of Our God and King"

Discuss: Thanking God

Read Psalm 8 to the Group. This psalm expresses the attributes of love. The psalms of praise give us a record of the way David and the prophet expressed their feelings to God. They can be read as a letter or as a monologue. Discuss this, and then read Psalm 150 in unison, as an act of thanks to God.

Next, divide into smaller groups of three or four, and assign each group three different psalms of praise from the list:

Psalm 19	Psalm 65	Psalm 96	Psalm 114
Psalm 24	Psalm 66	Psalm 97	Psalm 115
Psalm 29	Psalm 76	Psalm 99	Psalm 134
Psalm 33	Psalm 77	Psalm 104	Psalm 139
Psalm 47	Psalm 93	Psalm 111	Psalm 147
Psalm 50	Psalm 95	Psalm 113	Psalm 148

After the women have read over the psalms, suggest that they ask themselves some questions: Are all the psalms thankful? What is the writer thankful for? Are some requests mixed in with the thanks? Are the attributes of God listed? What are they? After ten or fifteen minutes, ask someone from each group to write their list, large enough for everyone to read, on sheets of newsprint which have been hung around the room. One list is of God's attributes; one is of things for which the writer was thankful. You may want to allow people to discuss their findings for a few minutes.

Closing Prayer

After the discussion, lead a prayer of thanks for the combined lists. For example:

O God, you are *all knowing,* we thank you for *guiding us;* you are *strong,* we thank you for *protecting us.* Amen.

Refreshments

DECEMBER

Objective

To gather for fellowship and rejuvenation during this busy time; to learn more about the sacred season and its symbols; to celebrate Advent together and look into the possibilities of winter.

Introduction

December comes from the Latin *decem*, or "tenth," relating to the month's placement in the old Julian calendar. The color is red, the flower is the poinsettia or holly, and the gem is turquoise. This month also brings the winter solstice—the shortest day of the year in terms of light hours; the earth is midway around the sun, headed back to more and more light.

Program

Gathering and Announcements

Tea/Fellowship Time

Symbols of Our Faith

Sing: "Prepare Ye the Way of the Lord"

Read: Isaiah 9:6-7; 35:1

Exhibit: The Christmas Rose
(display an ornament or picture)

The rose is common to Christian art. It symbolizes the promise of the Messiah.

Read: The story of the Christmas Rose

A helpful resource may be the book by James and Lillian Lewicki, *Golden Book of Christmas Tales: Legends from Many Lands* (New York: Simon & Schuster, 1956).

Sing: "Lo, How a Rose E'er Blooming"

Prayer

O Jesus, clear our minds and our vision so that we will recognize you in either the driest or the brightest spot. Use this season to prepare us. Make our hearts warm, our charity pure, and our hope strong enough to last through the bleak days of winter. Amen.

Decorating the Tree: Ornaments with a Meaning

Much is said about "keeping Christ in Christmas." In these days of fast-paced consumerism, it is easy to forget the original meaning of the day and the season.

One of the most familiar Christmas sights is the Christmas tree. The pine reflects the "evergreenness" of eternal life. During the Victorian era, the Christmas tree came into its fullest and most ornate state. A variation on this theme is the Chrismon tree, a combination of the words *Christ* and *monogram*.

All the ornaments are white, the season's liturgical color, and gold, signifying Christ's majesty and glory. All the designs are symbols of the Christian faith; some are the secret codes used by early Christians to communicate with one another during the days of persecution. The larger geometric forms also have symbolic meaning: the triangle stands for the trinity; the circle signifies eternal life; the combination of cross and globe symbolizes Christ's triumph over the world; the rectangle signifies Christ as the cornerstone of the Christian church.

Five-pointed Star: Called the star of Bethlehem or the star of Epiphany, this is the star that guided the wise men, representing the Gentiles. It is also a symbol of Mary—Mariam means "star." Read Matthew 2:1-2.

Scallop Shell: With drops of water falling from it, this represents John's baptism of Jesus. Read Mark 1:9-11.

Lamp or Candle: This symbolizes Christ as the Light of the world. Read John 8:12 and 9:5.

Fish: This is a symbol used by the early Christians to communicate secretly that the Lord's Supper would be celebrated in the home that evening. It may have been taken from Jesus' eating of fish after his resurrection. Read Luke 24:42.

IXΘYC: The Greek spelling of the word for fish, this served as an initialized code word for (J)esus (C)hrist, (G)od's (S)on, (S)avior.

ICHTHUS

Alpha and Omega: The first and last letters of the Greek alphabet symbolize the eternalness of Christ. Read Revelation 22:13.

Chi Rho: This abbreviation is one of the most ancient monograms used for Christ.

IHC: These are the first three letters of Jesus' name in Greek. Read Acts 4:12.

Butterfly: This symbol of the resurrection has life stages similar to those of the Christian. It begins as a worm, then passes through what seems to be death, to emerge in a new beautiful life-form.

Entwined Circles: This symbolizes the Trinity, the unity of three beings in one.

Crosses

Tau Cross: Named for the Greek letter it resembles, this probably was the shape of the cross on which Christ was crucified.

Latin Cross: This cross is the symbol of the risen and living Christ.

Passion Cross: With its sharp ends, this cross symbolizes Jesus' suffering and death.

Cross of Victory: This cross of world missions symbolizes the spread of Christ's message throughout the world.

Maltese Cross: This was the symbol of the Knights of Hospitality who guarded the pilgrims during the twelfth century. They lived on Malta after they were banished from Rhodes. The points symbolize the Beatitudes, joined at the center: Christ.

Jerusalem Cross: Four tau crosses joined at the base form this Crusader's cross. The center represents Mosaic law, and the four smaller crosses symbolize the four Gospels which displace that law. Some use it to represent the work of missions; the large cross represents the church and the four smaller crosses represent the four corners of the earth.

Invite the Women to Create Their Own Chrismons

Gather styrofoam or white cardboard, pearls, sequins, gold beads and glitter, glue, scissors, and straight pins. If possible, make up several ornaments before the meeting and bring a small real or artificial tree on which to display your ornaments. Choose six to ten symbols and make patterns or examples of them, then highlight each during the program.

After the program, invite the women to make ornaments of their own. Decide whether these will be used to decorate the church, be given as gifts to the homebound, or taken home to remind everyone of Christ's presence throughout the season.

Sing: "O Come, O Come, Emmanuel" as women gather their supplies. Then sing Christmas carols and enjoy fellowship as you work.

After about an hour, bring the meeting back to order and sing, "Hail to the Lord's Anointed."

Ask the women to come together and show their ornaments. If they are to be used in the church, hang them on the tree. If they are to be used in baskets for the homebound, place them in the baskets.

As a closing ritual, display a heart and describe its significance as the symbol of Christian love and service, because of its association with the center of the human impulse to help others.

Sing: "In the Bleak Midwinter"

Closing Prayer

O Prince of Peace, who came to us in a humble stable, we have made your symbols; we have talked of them and of you. And now our handicraft stands as our memory of this fellowship. Let the warmth of this room emanate into the winter world. Imprint the symbols on our hearts, that their meaning may be always present, always visible to the world around us. What can we give you? We give you our hearts. Amen.

Alternative Program

Use the beginning and closing devotions given and explore the many nativity paintings of Jesus from the perspective of artists around the world. Use books such as *The Faces of Jesus* (New York: Simon & Schuster, 1974). Sing "Some Children See Him," written by Alfred Burt.

How many different cultural adaptations can you find? How does it feel to see these unusual portrayals? This program might be embellished by having members make seasonal foods from around the world to bring to this meeting. Read some of the customs of each country as you eat the food or examine the picture from that country. A helpful resource may be Randolph Haughan's series, titled *An American Annual of Christmas Literature and Art* (Minneapolis: Augsburg, 1950s).

PROGRAMS WITH A THEME

Introduction

The four programs in this section revolve around specific themes: Lent, Prayer, Fellowship, and Missions. As noted in the heading of each program, they may be used as alternatives for the special days of the church women's calendar, or whenever the highlighted topic is relevant. These programs are planned as active meetings and work best with small groups of 75 or fewer people.

LENT

AN ALTERNATIVE PROGRAM
FOR THE CALL TO PRAYER AND SELF-DENIAL

Objective

To prepare for Lent, and to draw closer to God and to one another.

Program

Gathering and Announcements

Devotional Time

Text: John 8:3-11

Prayer: God of us all, we are sisters here. As we prepare for the coming of Easter's glory, help us to make sisters and brothers of the community and the world around us. Help us to reach out, rather than closing in upon ourselves. Help us to strive toward love instead of looking for fault. In the name of Christ, we pray. Amen.

The Old Grapevine

(Two women)

1: Hi, Beverly!
2: Hi, JoAnne, come in and sit down. How are you?
1: Oh, I'm just fine. I just came from the grocery.

2: Any good sales?

1: No. You know how food costs are. I think they can stuff $25 worth of groceries into a lunch sack anymore! I did see Mildred, though. That's why I stopped to talk to you.

2: M-M-M-M. What do you know that's new?

1: Well, I know that Mildred saw Sarah's daughter Julie coming in late again last night. It must have been around 3:00 A.M.!

2: Three o'clock in the morning!

1: Yes. Mildred was just getting up to get a drink of water when the car pulled in. She couldn't help noticing it.

2: Of course not. Mildred is a very sensitive person. Was it Sarah's car? I'm sure Julie is too young to drive.

1: No. A different car drops her off every night! Sometimes it's a real "treasure," according to Mildred—no muffler or anything. Mildred doesn't sleep well, anyway, since she broke her shoulder. This really has her upset!

2: A different car every night? I wonder what Sarah thinks. I'd surely be getting to the bottom of things!

1: Yes, I know you would, and so would I. But you know what kind of mother Sarah is—that nondirective parenting thing. You remember those camping disasters when we did the Girl Scout troop together? It was awful! That woman has no sense of *discipline* whatsoever.

2: JoAnne, your Melody used to be a close friend of Julie's, didn't she? Does Melody say anything about it?

1: No. Melody hardly sees Julie anymore. Julie rarely speaks when they meet in the hall. Melody says she looks tired and ragged when she does see her. I hate to think what *that* could mean. Do you think we should call the guidance counselor? Or should we talk with Reverend Sheen? What do you think, Beverly?

2: Well, we certainly must do something. It's our duty to the child. *Somebody* should help her. Heaven knows, it won't be Sarah!

1: Maybe I should call him and make an appointment.

2: No, I'll call. My phone is right here. You look over the newspaper while I call.

(Woman #2 leaves stage and goes off to make the call. Woman #1 picks up the newspaper and begins to leaf through it. Suddenly, she gasps and holds the paper away from her, calling.)

1. "Beverly, Beverly, hang up the phone!"
(Woman #2 comes back into the room.)
2: What's wrong, for heaven's sake?
1: Have you read the paper today?
2: No. I was just starting when you arrived. What is it?
1: Look at this!
2: Oh, my stars! It's Julie.
1: Go ahead, you might as well read it out loud.
2: "Area Girl Puts Courageous New Face on Candystriping. Julie Smail, 15, has been candystriping at St. Thomas Hospital for the past three years. Recently, when the hospital had its first two births of AIDS babies, Julie noticed that there weren't enough nurses to keep up with their needs. After a series of long, intense discussions, Julie persuaded the hospital to give her permission to stay after her regular shift to help in the nursery. Often, the nurses say, they are so understaffed that they fail to notice that Julie is still there until time for their early morning rounds. Nancy Kramer says that she and two of the other nurses often have to drag Julie away from the babies in order to drive her home. They are concerned about the toll this will take on Julie's sleep, but they admit they don't know what they would do without her help and love."
1: Beverly, I am so embarrassed. What a wonderful child. Such a compliment to Sarah's concern for the welfare of others. She must be very proud of having raised such a loving daughter.
2: I know what you mean, JoAnne. I'm surely glad the pastor didn't answer the phone. I left a message for him to call me back. I'll have to make up something when he calls.
1: Beverly?
2: Yes?
1: Well, I was thinking. It takes a lot of energy and commitment to do what Julie is doing. That's unusual devotion from a fifteen-year-old.
2: Yes, JoAnne?

1: Well, do you think Julie has any special reason for being so interested in those particular babies? I mean, read between the lines. Do you see anything *suspicious* here?
(Both women stop, look at the audience, and shrug.)

Discussion (leader)

The word *gossip* comes from an archaic word, *godsib*, literally, "one related to the gods." It was used in referring to middle-aged women of special wisdom. The word later developed into *gossip*, and during Elizabethian times meant "Godmother." In the centuries that followed, *gossip* came to mean one who spread community news, a "town crier." Only fairly recently has the word come to have negative connotations.

(Break into smaller groups of three or four, and give each group the following set of questions for discussion.)

1. What is the difference between "gossip" in the modern sense and "passing information"?

2. Have you ever helped to spread a rumor? How did you feel later? Was any damage done?

3. What effect did rumors have on Jesus' life? Read Luke 22:63-71 and 23:1-25.

4. How do we stop these rumors?

(Give the groups 10 to 12 minutes to discuss the questions, then call them back into a full group, and ask for any comments from the discussion. Then return to the Lenten theme.)

Preparing for Easter

We all give up something for Lent. It is common practice, or at least common conversation. Usually we think of giving up chocolate or television. In a more intentional way, we give up one meal every day and give the money to hunger projects.

Why not think about giving up something harmful to the Kingdom this Lent? We may not be gossips, but each of us spends some time making negative remarks about someone else, or about another group of people. Each time we do this, it drives a wedge between us—between God's people. And little by little, the dream of the Kingdom is lost.

Our negative comments and thoughts also drive wedges between ourselves and God. This Lent, let's give up the bad news and become spreaders of the Good News. And then, when Lent is over, we will be well-practiced bearers of the Good Tidings of the Resurrection.

Closing Prayer

Hear our confession, O Jesus. As we live through these days and moments of preparation for your return, help us to concentrate on the great love you had for all those you met—the tax collector, the adulteress, the poor. We remember the times when we judged instead of accepting, when we desired to be the first to tell the story, disregarding who would be hurt, when secrets slipped from our mouths before we noticed.

As we remind ourselves to center upon you during this time, remind us of the duty we have as sisters in your Kingdom. Open our ears, so we may hear the truth behind the insinuation. Open our arms, so we may embrace the world and those around us, that we may build up your Kingdom, rather than tearing it down. Amen.

Refreshments

PRAYER

AN ALTERNATIVE PROGRAM FOR WORLD DAY OF PRAYER

Objective

To learn more about prayer, to establish prayer partners and a prayer chain for the group and for the church.

Program

Gathering and Announcements

As each person enters, she is given an envelope holding the name of another member of the group. Ask the women to open the evelopes, find their partners, and sit with them during the program.

Devotions

Sing: "Standing in the Need of Prayer"

Read: The Vine and the Branches (John 15:1-8)

Pray

Loving God, we have prayed so many prayers over the years, yet we know so little about prayer. We ask, as the disciples asked Jesus: Teach us to pray. Teach us how better to communicate with you and with one another. Remind us to listen as well as to talk. Push us to acknowledge that prayer is as normal and natural a conversation mode as talking with our friends. Use our prayers. Unite their power into one large energy field of your love, so that through you, our love will be spread throughout the world. In Jesus' name, Amen.

Turn on the Power

The way we pray reflects the way we feel at that specific moment. Our prayers reflect our pains, our insecurities, our ambitions, our stubbornness, our independence. We push these things onto God, until God has no room to act, there is no room for God's abundance to flow over us. It is similar to our communication with our families. Sometimes we push so much talk at them, there is no room for them to respond. Prayer is dialogue. And dialogue always allows for both partners. And it always changes both partners.

Silence is also important. It is necessary for us to concentrate on God, not on who we think God is, or on our ideas and perceptions of God. We need to give God room for self-revelation. We need to give God room to transform us.

God never waits. The things for which we ask are always there. We must learn to be silent and patient enough to find them.
(The leader brings out a diagram of an electrical outlet.)

Prayer is an energy source, just like electricity. The reason we care so much about electricity is because of its power to do things. In what ways did you use electricity before you came to this meeting? I hope we feel the same way about prayer. I hope we use prayer as often.

We pray in order to communicate—to connect with that Great Power Source of the Creator. Just as we must plug into God, we must focus directly, in order for contact to be direct. Women may understand this better than men, for we are taught the importance of communication at an early age; we understand the power of verbal communication—talking, gabbing, shooting the breeze.

Not only must we plug in and connect, we also must work at it. Though electricity can power our lights, it also can shock us and cause fires. Have you ever examined the battery cables on a car engine? Mine are often corroded. My connection is weaker because I don't spend time keeping the cables clean. Prayer deserves our care, our time, our sincerity, our devotion. The line of communication must be kept strong. Frayed wires cause fires. Our line of communication to God must be solid for our message to get

98

through, and for us to trust it. Any form of communication is worthless without trust.

Prayer is communication. The connections must be direct and pure. We must listen—actively, and speak directly. We must listen both to ourselves and to God, just as we expect God to listen to us. We cannot afford to make assumptions about God's will. Neither can we afford to neglect the communication channels. God's love for us is secure. We need only learn to open the depths of our souls to God, and listen quietly and with patience. God is always there.

Group Discussion: Give the women a set of questions to work through with their prayer partners.

1. What does prayer mean to you?

2. Do you have a favorite prayer?

3. Do you remember a time when God was closer to you than at any other time? What happened? When do you feel closest to God? Most cut-off? Do you have any idea what causes the difference?

4. When do you feel closest to your family/friends?

5. What similarities exist between the way you talk with God and the way you talk with your closest friends/spouse?

6. Are there special things you want to learn or experience about prayer this year? Are there special prayers you will need this year?

7. How will you best use your prayer partner? Will you get together to pray every day, or once a week, or once a month? Would it be better to talk on the telephone? How often? What do you need from her? What are you willing to share with her? Will it be enough to remember her in your daily prayers and know that she is also naming you in hers? Make a covenant now with her—an agreement that meets the needs of both of you.

When the whole group has reassembled, ask if there are any questions or comments about the prayer partners' questions. If one is needed, form a prayer chain, have people write their names and phone numbers on the chalkboard, then link the names. Explain how to deal with the chain if someone is not home to receive a call. Promise to make a copy of the list to distribute at the next gathering or by mail. Discuss the importance of a prayer chain—the linking of power, one prayer multiplied exponentially.

The problems in need of prayer need no explanation. We need only pass on the first name of the person in need of prayer, and, if applicable, any specific time that the prayer is most needed—for example, during the hour of surgery.

Now take time to reflect. Prayer is a power force, very much like electricity. We must make sure that we are using it purely and always for good, for the positive. Prayer requires devotion and constant care. Ask if any favorite prayers were mentioned by their partners. If so, they may be used now. Ask whether there are any special concerns to be mentioned. Ask members to stand in a circle and hold hands to pray.

Closing Prayer

Holy Spirit, who binds us all together in this life, connect us now—to you and to one another. Increase our openness as we talk with you. Teach us to listen for your direction. Help us to trust you.

We lift to you those whose names have been mentioned, and we stop to mention our own . . . *(leader begins by stating her name, and it continues around the circle)*. We devote ourselves to a purer, clearer connection with you. Bind us to our prayer partners, so that we may truly communicate with one another and help each other to know you.

We pray for our church, our community, our nation, our world. Combine your power with ours to bring about justice and compassion, love and peace in this world. And, now we pray in the way Jesus taught . . . Our Father, who art in heaven . . . Amen.

Sing: "Every Time I Feel the Spirit"

Refreshments

Note: If this is a whole day, use some of the exercises found in the back of the book. You may also want to use some of the prayer resources found there. Read the parable of the persistent widow (Luke 18:1-8) and the parable of the Pharisee and the publican (Luke 18:9-14).

FELLOWSHIP

AN ALTERNATIVE PROGRAM
FOR MAY FELLOWSHIP DAY

Objective

To enjoy a time of community with other women, to acknowledge our God-given talents and abilities, to recognize our interdependence.

Program

Gathering and Announcements

Suggested Exercises: "Shakes," "Fitting In," "Mirror," "Hold On," "Drawing"

Sing: "We Are One in the Spirit, We Are One in the Lord"

Read: Parable of the Talents (Matthew 25:14-30)

Activity

Groups of three to five are assigned to read over Luke 19:11-27 and role-play it.

Comments About Talents (leader)

That is a familiar parable, told in two forms. It always reminds us that we do have talents and that we must use them. The results are a little threatening, intimating that unused talents are taken away. Even though such parables are familiar, each of us must begin with the admission that we have some very special God-given talents and abilities.

As women, we have been well schooled in humility. It has been said that women's original sin is not pride, but self-effacement. That is an area in which we need to work. The world needs our talents. God gave them to us for a purpose.

What would happen if we had to exhibit our talents in order to join the church? That's not so extreme. Clergy must discuss their gifts and graces for ministry. Some social agencies even screen their volunteers before asking them to serve. None of us needs to worry about whether we have any talents; we are amply supplied. What would happen, though, if we had to interview with a church official in the same way we must interview with a prospective employer? Wouldn't that be different? Let's take a look.

The Supreme Interview

(Two women are in an office setting with a desk and some files. Saint Margorie (M) is dressed in a white robe. Helen (H) is in street clothing, and is nervous.)

M: So, you want to join the church?

H: Yes, I hope to.

M: Well, what can you do for us?

H: Well, not much, really. I guess I'm kind of an ordinary woman, kind of simple, really.

M: Well, let me look. I'm sorry, Helen, but it says here that we have filled all our slots for simple, ordinary people. I'll keep your file on hand for one year. You may want to check back.

H: But I really want you to take me in. Can't you give me another chance?

M: All right, Helen. Do you have any special talents?

H: Well, nothing special. I like to sing a little.

M: Can you read music? We have an all-professional choir, you know.

H: No, I can't read music. But I have really good pitch.

M: Sorry, we don't need any more singers who can't read music. We're stock full.

H: But I'm pretty good. I can practice.

M: What else do you have?

H: Isn't that enough?

M: Listen, Honey, we get hundreds of applications in here every day. You saw the line when you came in. I'll have to see something pretty solid here!

H: OK, OK, . . . well, I'm a good reader.

M: Can you read loudly?

H: I'm a little timid, actually.

M: Sorry. We've got all the timid people we need.

H: Well, I can be pretty bold. I delivered the presentation speech at our awards dinner at work last year. I was pretty good.

M: I'm sorry. Pretty good just won't do.

H: Other people said I was really good.

M: What did you think?

H: Well, I . . . I thought I was real good, too.

M: Real good we've got plenty of room for. Now we're getting somewhere. I'll write that down. What else?

H: You need more?

M: That line outside is getting longer . . .

H: I know, I know. I've worked at the local food bank for ten years.

M: What do you do?

H: I keep the books.

M: Already got a bookkeeper. He likes to work alone.

H: I hire the employees.

M: That's *my* job, and I'm not retiring for a long time.

H: And I fill the members' needs.

M: Filling members' needs. Now, that's something a church's got plenty of room for. How did you start at the food bank?

H: Actually, I helped to organize it in the first place.

M: Oh, that's interesting. How did that happen?

H: Several of us who had been working on hunger issues for a long time got so angry about the waste of food in our restaurants and grocery stores that we decided to talk with the managers. They had nothing to lose, so they began to give us their damaged goods and leftovers. We took it to the agencies that fed people. Soon, we were getting so many donations that we had to start storing it.

M: Where'd you put it all?

H: First we put it in my freezer, but that wasn't big enough for long, so I asked warehouses to lend us space until we could afford to rent our own little warehouse.

M: You're really a mover and shaker. That's quite an accomplishment.

H: Five of us worked on it together. Three of them have moved on to other issues now, so we've had to hire staff to help.

M: And you run this program?

H: Well, yes, but it's small, not like in the big cities.

M: Watch it, you're backsliding. You don't want to play fast and easy with these God-given abilities, child. You have them for a reason. Don't go apologizing on God! It doesn't go over too well.

H: You're right. Sorry.

M: So, instead of a simple ordinary kind of woman here, we have a woman who can see a community need and respond to it in an effective way. And, a woman who sticks with it. The singing just gets thrown in as an extra. Keep practicing—that singing will save you on some of those long days. I guess you're in, Kiddo. Take this paper to the woman behind the window. And, ah, would you send the next one in as you leave?

H: Thanks.

M: Don't thank me, Honey. *I* didn't give you those talents. Just don't waste them.

H: You bet.

(The women exit.)

Group Response

(Have sheets of newsprint hanging on the walls; supply markers for the women to use in listing their talents.)

The moral is: Don't underestimate your gifts. What gifts do *you* have? Go to one of the newsprint sheets you see around the room, and list some of your talents and abilities.

Sing: "Many Gifts, One Spirit"

Comments (leader)

Now let's look at our interdependence. When we accept our talents, sometimes we think that we must tackle everything alone. We are not alone. Look around the room at all the talents and abilities represented in this group. Just think what we can do when we share all of this!

Read: 1 Corinthians 12:12

Exercises: "Massage," "Group Pantomime," "Helping," "Gifts"
(You may want to include "Fall")

Sing: "Simple Gifts" (" 'Tis the gift to be simple . . . ")

Prayer

Creator of us all, our gifts do not belong to us, but to you. Remind us of those things that make us unique in your Kingdom. When we try to take on the world alone, remind us of the interdependence of your whole creation. Love us through our limitations, and help us to live with them. Inspire us to recognize our talents—to use them and develop them and share them. Make us your lights in a world that sometimes is so dark. In Christ's name, Amen.

Sing: "This Little Light of Mine"

Refreshments

MISSIONS

AN ALTERNATIVE PROGRAM
FOR WORLD COMMUNITY DAY

Objective

To remember our ministry to the world, to broaden our understanding of the world's problems and the programs serving to meet them, to commit ourselves to action in today's world.

Program

Gathering and Announcements

(Methodist Bishop McConnell's mother referred to people who didn't believe that religion has anything to do with politics or social issues as "soft heads.")

Devotions

Read: Luke 4:18-19

Sing: "The Voice of God Is Calling"

Activity

(Clip one news article about each of the following problems from a current newspaper or magazine. The article may highlight either the problem or a hopeful solution that is being tried. Intersperse these with the scripture texts. Ask various women to read them aloud; preferably, the odd number items should be read from one side of the room and the even numbered items from the other side.)

1. Poverty Article
2. Amos 8:4-11
3. Hunger Article

6. Mark 10:17-22
7. Prejudice Article
8. Ephesians 2:13-18

4. II Samuel 12:1-6   9. Disease article
5. Homelessness article   10. Luke 16:19-31

Sing: "Where Cross the Crowded Ways of Life"

Read

What is mission? Simply put, mission is remaining close to God, open to God's leading, sensitive to God's caring, and knowledgeable of God's constant working through history to benefit the poor, the hungry, the homeless, the disinherited and outcast, the sick. Being in mission is being aware that God's devotion is never changing, but God's methods are ever fresh, ever new, ever ready to combat new pains and struggles. Whenever we think we have God's will all caged up in a box, neatly wrapped, God's directions change. Mission is listening with ears sensitized by God's concern for humanity—listening intently, then acting decisively and without regret.

Sing: "Be Thou My Vision"

Read: Luke 4:16-21 (First woman reads verses 16-17; three women read 18-19; third woman reads 20-21.)

Sing: "O Young and Fearless Prophet"

Read: Carl Sandburg's poem "Mag"

Sing: "What Child Is This?"

Read: W. H. Auden's poem:

Hunger allows no choice to the citizen or the police;
We must love one another or die.

Sing: "O Holy City Seen of God"

Read: John 21:13-17

Group Participation

Ask the women to call out groups of people who are hurting, making a list on chalkboard or sheet of newsprint. Use these in the prayer. (Examples: Haitians, people living with AIDS, the homeless)

Pray

O Lord, today, you are *Haitian*. Teach us how to help you.
O Lord, today, you are *living with AIDS*. Teach us how to help you.
(Repeat until the whole list has been prayed for; conclude with "Amen.")

Sing: "Kum Ba Yah, My Lord"

Read: Luke 4:18-19

Pray

O God of the Abundant Harvest, you are ours, and we have so much. Remind us that you also are the God of the needy. You hear their concerns, their needs, their fears. The faces we see on the nightly news, the lives described in our daily papers, the people we pass on our sidewalks and see in our missions—all these belong to you. The cries of the world go out every moment of every day. And they all go out to you.

Often, there seems so little we can do. Transform us, Lord, into people who turn their prayers into action, their thanks into concern for others. Teach us what to do, Lord, that we might be saved. Amen.

Sing: "Lord, Whose Love Through Humble Service"

Refreshments

ADDITIONAL RESOURCES

Introduction

This section contains additional resources to be used as suggested or to develop specific themes. The quizzes for Black History Month and Women's History Month may be used as suggested or printed as facts for information or discussion.

The warm-up exercises included are divided into five groups, arranged in order of increasing difficulty in terms of acting ability or physical movement:

1. Warm-up Exercises
2. Icebreakers
3. Group Building
4. Creativity Development.

Use these excercises playfully, and without strain, or choose your own with which you feel more comfortable.

The selected list of suggested resources is provided merely for supplemental material.

Exercises

Warm-up Exercises

1. Shakes

Have the group stand where they have plenty of room. After they stretch in every direction, ask them to shake their entire bodies, starting with the left arm and continuing until every part of the body is involved. When everyone is shaking all over, ask them to say "Ah" out loud as they continue to shake. After one minute, ask them to bend forward, then backward, then sideways while shaking, then stop.

2. Massage

Have the group stand in a straight line. Ask them to turn to the person on their right and massage her neck and back for one minute. Next, have them turn to the person on their left and massage her neck and back for one minute.

3. Pulling Together

Have the group stand and shake arms, legs, and necks. Ask them to find partners and face them. Then join left hands and pull in opposite directions. Switch hands and repeat. Do this twice.

4. Side Stretch

Ask the women to find partners. Each couple stands back to back, with arms linked tightly. Ask the couples to bend over and touch the floor to the right of them, then stand up straight. Then bend over and touch the floor to the left, then stand up straight. Repeat twice.

5. Keystone Cops Rag

The group stands and stretches, bending down, twisting, jumping up and down. Ask for a volunteer to be "it." Ask the group to run around the room at an easy pace, in a regular game of tag, trying to avoid "it." After one minute, blow a whistle and tell them to move in slow motion. After two minutes, blow the whistle again and ask them to rush, taking baby steps and imitating the early silent movies. After two minutes, blow the whistle again, telling them to go back to the normal pace. Repeat until everybody has mastered the movement.

Icebreakers

1. Getting to Know You

Instruct the group to form a circle. Supply a volleyball or some comparable object. Ask the members to toss the ball from person to person. As each one catches the ball, she must yell out her name, then throw the ball.

2. Mystery Identity

Before the group arrives, print the names of members on note cards. As each person arrives, tape a note card on her back. Each woman must guess whose name is on the note card she has by asking "yes" or "no" questions of the other members.

3. Fitting In

Divide the group in half. Mask off two squares on the floor. Ask the groups to stand in the squares. They must all get in and stay within the square, without any part of their bodies protruding. The team that can hold this position longest wins.

4. Mirror

Have the group stand and stretch. Ask them to choose a partner and face her. Touch finger tips and move hands in a circular motion. Look into each other's eyes for one minute. Repeat this action once. Next, have one woman pretend to be waking up. Ask her partner to mimic her actions. Have the other woman mime getting dressed. Have her partner mimic her actions.

Group Builders

1. Guess the Leader

One or more people volunteer to be "it." While the volunteer(s) leave the room, the group chooses a leader. When "it(s)" return, the group copies the movements of the leader, changing them whenever the leader changes. "It(s)" must learn the identity of the leader.

2. Blindfolded

Have the group stand and shake their whole bodies. Ask them to close their eyes. They then move around the room, bumping into one another. Do this for five minutes. (It will be necessary to clear the room of any hazards and have troubleshooters watching, so that no one wanders too far away or into danger.)

3. Hold On

Have the group stand in a straight line. The leader stretches a rope from the first person to the last, asking each woman to hold the rope with both hands and close their eyes. The leaders must guide the group, instructing the women where to walk—warning of rough places, turns, and so on. When the group returns to the starting place, they stop and open their eyes.

4. Follow the Leader

The group stands in a large circle. Thin sticks are distributed, and the women hold these between them, forming one large connected circle. The leader drops one hold, breaking the connection, and proceeds to lead the group over and through the other sticks, until the group is thoroughly entangled. Without letting go of the sticks, the group must figure out how to untangle themselves.

5. Fall

The group stands in a close circle, facing inward. Ask members to hold hands tightly. One person stands in the center and closes her eyes, letting herself fall backward. As the woman falls, the group members support her. This continues until each woman has been in the center.

Creativity Development

1. Drawing

Divide the group into small groups and have them sit with their backs to one another. Distribute pencils, some blank cards, and a card imprinted with a simple design. Have one member describe the design to the others, while they attempt to draw it on their cards. The woman doing the describing may not show the design to the others, and they cannot ask questions. Repeat until all have described a design.

2. Group Pantomime

Divide into smaller groups. Using note cards, assign an activity for each group to act out in pantomime (for example: a canoe ride through rapids, a game of bridge). When each group has finished, ask them to be seated and watch as the other groups perform.

3. Helping

The group stands in a circle, facing inward. One person goes to the center and performs a task (for example, sawing wood). As the other members decide what the person in the center is pantomiming, she joins in to "help" accomplish the task (for example: bringing more wood, supporting the piece being sawed).

4. Gifts

Provide a box of trinkets (for example: old handkerchiefs, worn-out gloves, bubble fluid). Instruct each woman to choose an object and decide upon a way to make it a gift to another member of the group (for example: blow a bubble, wipe her forehead).

Quizzes

Black Americans in History:
Do You Know Who . . .

1. The first black to win the U.S. Open at Forest Hills. He began tennis at age 7; his serve was his "deadliest weapon."

2. Frustrated with public schools, this teacher won national recognition for starting her own, taking children back to the basics.

3. The first black American in space, he was launched in 1983 aboard Shuttle Challenger No. 8. He conducted experiments in space which helped in treating diabetes.

4. She was the first black woman to make the nonfiction best-seller list for her autobiography, *I Know Why the Caged Bird Sings*, and the first black woman to have an original screenplay produced (she directed it, too!). She sings, and has been active in the Southern Christian Leadership Conference for civil rights.

5. With an honorable discharge from the Air Force, he still needed the aid of President Kennedy, 500 U.S. marshals, and 20,000 troops, to enter the University of Mississippi in 1962. He later earned his law degree from Columbia University.

6. He is the youngest person ever to win a Nobel Peace Prize. He had a dream and a nonviolent way of achieving it.

7. He was the first black man in organized baseball.

8. After working all day as a seamstress, she was too tired to move to the back of the bus. Her arrest began the 381-day bus strike in Alabama.

9. Quite a prima donna of the opera, she sang in the church choir at age 9, then won a scholarship to Julliard. In 1961, her debut made her the first black to open a Metropolitan Opera season.

10. As chairperson of the NAACP, this famous scholar established the Springarn Gold Medal for the noblest achievement by a black American.

11. A famous writer and philosopher, his best known work was *The Souls of Black Folk.* With William Monroe Trotter, he founded the Niagara Movement, which became the NAACP.

12. Born into slavery, he became an agricultural genius and scientist, as well as accomplished pianist, and was honored on a postage stamp in 1948. In 1973, he was elected to the Hall of Fame of Great Americans.

13. She was a great orator and activist for the rights of blacks, children, women, and laborers. She traveled over the country making speeches and helping people.

14. The man who invented the first electric light bulb with carbon filament, he gave Edison the idea for developing the modern electric light.

15. This woman spoke strongly against lynching, even after the opposition burned down her newspaper building. She was an advocate of civil rights and suffrage.

16. A musical genius, he wrote and played tunes which sold millions.

17. A true freedom fighter, she helped more then 300 slaves flee to Canada. At one time, $40,000 was offered for her capture. A master of disguise, she was called Moses.

18. A brilliant surgeon, he founded Provident Hospital, the first interracial hospital in America, and the first training school for black nurses.

19. With his brother J. Rosamond, he wrote more than 200, songs including "Lift Ev'ry Voice and Sing," which became the black national anthem. He founded the first black daily newspaper and served as Consul to Venezuela and Nicaragua 1906–1912.

20. She served as a U.S. representative from Texas. She was a powerful member of the Judiciary Committee, a champion of civil rights, an educator, and an able constitutional lawyer.

21. His novels and essays are both strong and sensual. The eldest of nine children growing up in Harlem, his work was read and honored all over the world.

22. She was the first black to win at Wimbledon in 1957. It was only her second try.

23. An ordained minister and leader in the Southern Christian Leadership Conference, he was the first black U.N. ambassador from the U.S.

24. A tall, 200-pound pioneer, she worked in a mission in Montana, drove a mail wagon, and toted a .38 under her apron.

25. An abolitionist, a profound orator and leader, he advised President Lincoln. This ex-slave toured England to speak of the evils of slavery, and started a newspaper, *The North Star.*

26. He was a legend cowboy: a roper and shooter in the rodeo.

27. The son of a Baptist minister, he played the organ at the age of 12; he sold more than 25 million records. He was the first black to host a nationally broadcast television show.

28. She was elected to represent New York, the first black woman in Congress. She campaigned for president in 1972.

29. He was a famous tap dancer and actor, known to many as Bojangles. He starred with Shirley Temple.

30. He reached the North Pole 45 minutes before Admiral Perry. He was famous as a polar explorer.

31. He was the first black actor to play Othello on an American stage. He spoke all the modern languages and could read twenty. He was a brilliant actor and civil rights leader.

32. The "Empress of the Blues," she began her career in 1923 and became an overnight star, but died following an automobile crash because the white hospital denied care.

33. Born on July 4, he began his career from the Colored Home for Waifs and bought his first horn for just ten dollars. He played command solos for King George V; folks called him Satchmo.

34. He was working as a soda jerk when he wrote his first hit. He started piano lessons at age 7, but wouldn't practice; he recorded radio shows from Harlem's Cotton Club, and some of his hits were written in just 20 minutes.

35. The 15th of 17 children, she went to school between cotton-picking seasons. With a scholarship, she studied to be a missionary, but opened a school instead, selling cakes and ice cream to support it. She served as president when the school became Bethune-Cookman College.

36. At age 6, she sang at a Baptist church to pay for her singing lessons; in 1939, she was barred from singing at Constitution Hall, but in 1958, she was the first black to sing at the Metropolitan in New York.

37. She gave up her singing career to work with her husband, but toured the U.S. and India, giving concerts and working for civil rights and against nuclear arms. After the assassination of her husband, she built a Center for Nonviolent change.

38. As President Carter's Secretary of HUD, she was the first black woman to hold a top Cabinet post. She served as ambassador to Luxembourg, the first black woman to head an American embassy.

39. Her determination to vote cost her her job in Mississippi, but in 1964, she led the black delegates from Mississippi to the Democratic National Convention.

40. A poet and novelist who got his start writing for a high school paper in Cleveland, he was discovered by Vachel Lindsay while serving as a busboy. (He placed his poems on Lindsay's plate.)

41. An educator and a surgeon, his research in blood plasma led to the first blood bank in 1940, saving scores of lives in World War II. He died after an accident, having been denied access to the plasma in a white hospital.

42. A political scientist and educator, he worked as the State Department's first black official, taking over as the U.S. mediator in Jerusalem in 1948; he received the Nobel Peace Prize in 1955, the first black to do so.

43. The grandson of a slave, he was asked by the NAACP to be their assistant general counsel; he won the classic school-desegregation case on May 15, 1954. The first black to be appointed to the U.S. Supreme Court, he was known as Mr. Civil Rights.

44. A dancer and choreographer, she began dancing at age 9 and gave dancing lessons to put herself through school. She studied dance all over the world and was a great philanthropist.

45. She began writing at age 7, and later succeeded Carl Sandburg as the Illinois poet laureate; she was the first black woman to win the Pulitzer Prize.

46. He was the first American to win four Olympic Gold Medals (1936). A sickly child born to a sharecropper, his 5th-grade coach encouraged him to run.

47. As president of the Arkansas NAACP in 1954 when the Supreme Court ruled against segregation in the schools, she pushed the Little Rock school board to develop a plan. When Eisenhower sent troops, the Governor closed the schools. In 1958, the Circuit Court of Appeals opened them again.

48. The son of a Baptist minister, the KKK burned his house and killed his father; as a Black Muslim, he encouraged black self-assertion; he later broke with the Muslims to form the Organization of Afro-American Unity; a brilliant speaker, he was assassinated at age 39.

49. He blended traditional black church music with the blues to become the Father of Gospel Music; he wrote "Precious Lord" and more than 900 others.

50. America's Ambassador of Love, she toured vaudeville and the USO; an actress, singer, and theologian, she starred in *Hello Dolly* and served as an advisor to the U.N. delegation.

Answers to the Black Americans in History Quiz:

1. Arthur Ashe
2. Marva Collins
3. Lt. Col. Guion S. Bluford, Jr.
4. Marguerite Johnson, "Maya Angelou"
5. James Meredith
6. Dr. Martin Luther King, Jr.
7. Jackie Robinson
8. Rosa Parks
9. Leontyne Price
10. Dr. Joel E. Spingarn
11. W. E. B. DuBois
12. Dr. George Washington Carver
13. Sojourner Truth
14. Lewis H. Latime

15. Ida B. Wells-Barnett
16. Scott Joplin
17. Harriet Tubman
18. Dr. Daniel H. Williams
19. James Weldon Johnson
20. Barbara Jordon
21. James Baldwin
22. Althea Gibson
23. Andrew Young
24. Mary Fields, "Black Mary"
25. Frederick Douglass
26. Nat Love, "Deadwood Dick"
27. Nat "King" Cole
28. Shirley Chisholm
29. Bill Robinson
30. Matthew Attenson
31. Paul Robeson
32. Bessie Smith
33. Louis Armstrong
34. "Duke" Ellington
35. Mary McCleod Bethune
36. Marion Anderson
37. Coretta Scott King
38. Patricia Harris
39. Fannie Lou Hamer
40. Langston Hughes
41. Dr. Charles Drew
42. Dr. Ralph Bunche
43. Thurgood Marshall
44. Katherine Dunham
45. Gwendolyn Brooks
46. Jesse Owens
47. Daisy Bates
48. Malcolm X
49. Thomas Dewey
50. Pearl Bailey

Which American Woman Was It Who . . .

1. Ran away from marriage in Canada, then dressed as a soldier and enlisted in the Civil War?

2. Defended civil-rights cases in the 1950s, acted in peace and women's movements in the 1960s, and won a seat in the U.S. House in the 1970s. She also founded the National Women's Caucus?

3. Founded the Feminist Studio Workshop, attacked social taboos through her art, and created *The Dinner Party* to honor 999 women?

4. Was rejected for employment by private law firms when she graduated from Stanford, and later became the first woman justice on the United States Supreme Court?

5. Was the eldest of four daughters and became the sole bread-winner when her father's school closed; she wrote poems, essays, and novels, including *Little Women,* to support her family?

6. Published articles on temperance, social reform, women's suf-frage, education, and property law, and supported the first woman to defy the dress code, when she herself donned a pair of bloomers?

7. Labored tirelessly for passage of the 19th Amendment until it passed in 1920, then founded the League of Women Voters?

8. Was better known as Mother Jones, worked for the rights of immigrant laborers and against deportation; she founded the American Civil Liberties Union?

9. Wrote a poem that was chosen over those of Twain, Whit-man, Harte, and Longfellow for inscription on the Statue of Liberty?

10. Was elected to the governor's post in Connecticut in 1974, the first woman elected in her own right, and ran her office from the hospital room where she was being treated for cancer?

11. Won four academy awards for her roles, a strong and inde-pendent actress whose most frequent co-star was Spencer Tracy?

12. Was an economist and writer who attacked women's finan-cial dependency, pushed for centralized nurseries and coopera-tive kitchens, she put her Utopian dream in a novel titled *Herland?*

13. Fought social injustice and private pain through her plays; was a daring writer who was questioned during the McCarthy era?

14. From being the first woman director of the New York Stock Exchange, became the first woman Secretary of Commerce; she was concerned with labor, and with equality based on race, sex, and age?

15. Began painting as a hobby when she was 57, was "discovered" at age 68, and had her first solo show at age 80; she produced 2,000 paintings of American country life?

16. Was a temperance reformer, smashing bottles and saloons with an axe as she preached and sang hymns?

17. Began in medical school, but fell in love with air flight as a new opportunity for women, she did mechanical and physiological studies, but never returned from her transworld flight in 1937?

18. Was trained for the opera, but fell in love with folk music; she worked in a button factory to pay for her music lessons and wound up at Carnegie Hall?

19. A true markswoman, she shot game to support her family after her father's death; she toured with the "Wild Bill" Hickok show, and once shot a cigarette from the mouth of Kaiser William II?

20. Designed patterns for lace and embroidery until Alfred Steiglitz exhibited her work in his studio; she is best known for her studies of flowers and the Southwest.

21. Ran a bookstore and publishing house frequented by Hawthorne; she wrote educational texts, established the first public kindergarten, and campaigned for education for Native Americans?

22. Organized the National Women's Party in 1918 to fight for an Equal Rights Amendment; she also fought for pacifism and for a public role for women?

23. She was a feminist and journalist, but was famous for her clairvoyance. She and her sister had such an effect on Cornelius Vanderbilt that he established them as the first professional female stockbrokers?

24. As a teacher and a Senator from Maine, she was almost nominated for President in 1964, but came in second to Barry Goldwater; she remained a senator until the age of 74 and later served as a syndicated columnist?

25. Also known as Lt. Harry Buford, dressed as a man and joined her husband in the Civil War; she was wounded at the battle of Bull Run and later stole behind Union lines as a spy?

26. Was a caseworker for the New York Welfare Department and worked on voter registration; wrote *The Color Purple,* which became a theme book for women of color, feminists, and theologians alike?

27. She investigated the connection between poverty and infant/maternal death, campaigned for birth control, founded 80 clinics, and was the first president of the International Planned Parenthood Federation in 1953?

28. Born a slave and educated in freedman's schools, she was driven from Memphis in 1892 because of her antilynching editorials; in Chicago, she co-founded the NAACP, worked in civil rights, and began the first black suffrage association?

29. An ecologist and scientist, she was awarded for her writing on irresponsible pesticide use and her warnings about industrial growth; in 1962, she wrote *Silent Spring*?

30. An investigative journalist, branded a "muckraker" by Teddy Roosevelt, she campaigned against corruption and big-business interests; President Wilson sent her to the Industrial Conference, and President Harding sent her to the Unemployment Conference?

31. The nurse who drove a mule team during the Civil War to deliver supplies bought by her own money; in 1881, she organized the American Red Cross; she again drove a mule team to the soldiers during the Spanish-American War, when she was 77 years old?

32. Organized the International Ladies' Garment Union in 1915 and worked to unite the laborers with the middle-class reformers; she organized Bryn Mawr's summer schools for women workers in 1921 and fought for education, the eight-hour day, and minimum wage?

33. The Congresswoman from New York who was nominated for Vice President on the Democratic Ticket in 1984?

34. Using the name Nelly Bly, she wrote of slum life, asylum conditions, sweat shops, and crime, while operating undercover; she went around the world in 72 days, stopping to interview Jules Verne en route?

35. Dressed as a man to have greater freedom, she enlisted as a soldier to earn money; she was wounded in battle with the British and received an honorable discharge?

36. Developed surgery to relieve "Blue Baby" death in 1944; she discovered the advantages of X-ray in diagnosing heart and lung problems, and recognized the dangers of thalidomide in 1962; in 1959, she became the first female full professor at Johns Hopkins Medical School?

37. Her father was a friend of Lincoln; she withdrew from medical school due to a serious spinal problem and founded the Settlement House Movement to create a protective human community in the city; used political action to overcome class barriers and social injustice, and won the Nobel Peace Prize in 1931?

38. Became blind and deaf at 19 months of age; through her teacher, learned to speak, to read braille, and had all her college lectures tapped out in her hand; spoke fluent French and German, and studied the classics; swam, rode, and typed her own papers; raised $2,000,000 for the American Foundation for the Blind through her lecture tour; resented all forms of condescension to the differently abled?

39. Made anthropology accessible to the common person, and her studies were widely read; used her skills to mediate between nations during World War II; helped people understand their own culture by understanding those of others?

40. Wrote *Feminine Mystique* in 1963 about suburban life among wives, calling it "the problem which has no name," and became known as the "mother of the new feminism"; helped found the First Women's Bank?

Which American Woman Was It Who—Quiz Answers

1. Sarah Edwards
2. Bella Abzug
3. Judy Chicago
4. Sandra Day O'Connor

5. Louisa May Alcott
6. Amelia Bloomer
7. Carrie Chapman Catt
8. Elizabeth Gurley Flynn
9. Emma Lazarus
10. Ella Grasso
11. Kathryn Hepburn
12. Charlotte Perkins Gilman
13. Lillian Hellman
14. Juanita Kreps
15. Anna Mary Moses
16. Carrie Nation
17. Amelia Earhart
18. Odetta Gordon
19. Annie Oakley
20. Georgia O'Keeffe
21. Elizabeth Peabody
22. Alice Paul
23. Victoria Woodhull
24. Margaret Chase Smith
25. Loretta Velasquez
26. Alice Walker
27. Margaret Sanger
28. Ida Wells-Barnett
29. Rachel Carson
30. Ida Tarbell
31. Clara Barton
32. Rose Schneiderman
33. Geraldine Ferraro
34. Elizabeth Seaman
35. Deborah Sampson
36. Helen Taussig
37. Jane Addams
38. Helen Adams Keller
39. Margaret Mead
40. Betty Goldstein Friedan

PRAYER RESOURCES AND USEFUL BOOKS

African American History

Lee, George E. *Interesting People: Black American History Makers.* New York: Ballentine Books, 1989.

Christian Art, Illustrations, Diagrams

McGee, Ratha Doyle. *Symbols and Signposts of Devotion.* Nashville: The Upper Room, 1956.

Music

The United Methodist Hymnal. Nashville: The United Methodist Publishing House, 1989.

Prayers and Readings

DuBois, W. E. B. *Prayers for Dark People.* Amherst: University of Massachusetts Press, 1980.

Green, Barbara, and Victor Gollancz, eds. *God of a Thousand Names: Prayers and Meditations from Many Faiths and Cultures.* Oxford: Isis Large Print, 1986.

Harkness, Georgia. *Prayer and the Common Life.* Nashville: Abingdon Press, 1949.

Paton, Alan. *Instrument of Thy Peace: The Prayer of St. Francis of Assisi.* New York: Phoenix Press, 1984.

_____. *Peacemaking: Day by Day.* Erie, Penna.: Pax Christi USA, 1985.

Peitsch, William V. *The Serenity Prayer Book.* San Francisco: Harper & Row, 1990.

Redding, David A. *Before You Call I Will Answer.* Old Tappan, N. J.: Fleming H. Revell, 1985.

_____. *The Prayers I Love.* San Francisco: Strawberry Hill Press, 1978.

Roberts, Elizabeth, and Elias Amidon, eds. *Earth Prayers from Around the World.* San Francisco: Harper & Row, 1991.

Söelle, Dorothee. *Revolutionary Patience.* Maryknoll, N.Y.: Orbis Books, 1969.

Women's History

Ruether, Rosemary Radford, and Rosemary Skinner Keller. *Women in American Religion.* San Francisco: Harper & Row, 1981.

Uglow, Jennifer S., ed. *The International Dictionary of Women's Biography.* New York: Continuum Publishing Company, 1982.